Praise for
God on Pap...

"If you've got your bags packed and are ready to go and incarnate the gospel in this culture, think again. Better let the books in the Dialogue of Faith series rearrange what you take with you. Already this series has shown me my desperate need to unpack some baggage and repack for the challenges of tomorrow."

> —LEONARD SWEET, author of *Out of the Question…Into the Mystery*

"*God on Paper* gently and passionately tells God's Big Story. The beauty of Scripture is intensified through the author's dialogue with his conversation partner, Darius. This is much more than a book of great stories (though it is filled with them!)—it paints The Story."

> —MARK OESTREICHER, president of Youth Specialties

"Here is the compelling tale of the greatest love story ever told. Bryan Loritts shares God's love in a real and winsome way—a way that encourages and inspires, yet creates tension as he examines who God is and why He desires a relationship with us. This book will help you tell The Story to others."

> —DENNIS RAINEY, author and president of FamilyLife

"Bryan Loritts's conversation with Darius demonstrates that the reality of God, His story, and the gospel of Jesus Christ must be sent and received in different ways in every generation. The natural weaving of the biblical text with story and everyday life connects with a rapidly growing number of people who best receive God's truth through relationship."

> —TIM OSBORN, lead pastor of Warehouse at Lake Avenue Church, Pasadena, California

"God's activity in human history comes alive as you read these pages. Your heart will be warmed and deeply moved by this portrait of authentic Christianity and by the depths of God's love and passion for people!"
—Dr. Crawford W. Loritts Jr., speaker, author, and radio host

GOD
ON PAPER

dialogue
of faith

GOD
ON PAPER

THE BIBLE—THE WILDEST STORY
OF PASSION AND PURSUIT
YOU'LL EVER READ

 by BRYAN C. LORITTS

WATERBROOK
PRESS

GOD ON PAPER
PUBLISHED BY WATERBROOK PRESS
2375 Telstar Drive, Suite 160
Colorado Springs, Colorado 80920
A division of Random House, Inc.

The author has made every effort to ensure the truthfulness of the stories and anecdotes in this book. In a few instances, names and identifying details have been changed to protect the privacy of the persons involved.

ISBN 1-57856-790-4

Published in association with the literary agency of Alive Communications, Inc., 7680 Goddard Street, Suite 200, Colorado Springs, Colorado 80920.

Library of Congress Cataloging-in-Publication Data
Loritts, Bryan.
    God on paper : the wildest story of passion and pursuit you'll ever read / Bryan Loritts.
        p. cm.
    Includes bibliographical references.
    ISBN 1-57856-790-4
    1. God—Love—Biblical teaching. 2. Bible—Theology. I. Title.
BS544.L67 2005
231'.6—dc22   2004017407

Printed in the United States of America
2005—First Edition

10 9 8 7 6 5 4 3 2 1

To my wife, Korie—
the inspiration for this book.

To my children, Quentin and Myles—
May your faith be your own.

To Shiria and Nehru—
I hope this helps.

CONTENTS

ACKNOWLEDGMENTS

Whenever I watch an awards show on television and hear the elated artists thanking people, I know someone is going to be offended because his or her name was not mentioned. There's always that rub between not wanting to offend and wanting to express sincere and appropriate gratitude. So here goes...

My wife, Korie, has been so amazing. I know that's the politically correct thing to say, but it's also true. I'm a blessed man because I have a wife who prays for me and who frees me to fulfill God's calling on my life. Thanks, sweetheart.

This book could not have been written unless it came from my love for God's Word. The seeds for this romance were placed in my heart from the times when our family sat around the dinner table and listened to my father, Dr. Crawford Loritts Jr., read from God's Word. I am blessed to have a dad who hasn't just read and preached the Bible—he has lived it. Thanks, Dad, I love you. My West Coast dad (as I call him), Dr. Kenneth Ulmer, pastor of the Faithful Central Bible Church in Inglewood, California, has had a profound, indescribable influence on my life. Charles Brooks is another mentor who has really helped me understand a lot about God, especially his grace. Thanks for your unconditional love for me, and for not giving up on me.

Dr. E. Glenn Wagner, who asked me to be a part of the Dialogue of Faith project, is another man whose love for God and his Word has been a source of inspiration. Glenn, thanks for your influence as well as the opportunity.

Pastor Jody Moore, Dr. Johnny Baylor, Kirk Scott, and Dante Upshaw have been dear brothers to me. They continue to push me in my journey with God, helping fan the flames of passion for him. We've prayed together, cried together, and done life together. I'm a blessed man to have friends like you.

My teammates at Fellowship Bible Church Memphis—John Bryson, Kirk Scott, Ben Parkinson, and Tony Kim—have contributed significantly to my understanding of ministry and this mystery called the church. They've become brothers as we have ventured out on the trail of church planting. As John would say, "I'm glad you're in the bunker with me." I can't wait to see what the years ahead will bring. I also thank you guys and our church for giving me time to work on this project and sharing me with the body of Christ at large. Tony, I'll write my next book on War Hammer!

People such as Kyle Young, Jeff Mattesich, Jared Nelson, Jason Djang, and a host of others have sharpened my thinking, particularly on the subjects of Scripture and postmodernism. Thanks for the late-night discussions and the e-mail conversations.

Ron Lee and the staff at WaterBrook Press have been beyond huge in sifting through my manuscript and helping make changes while maintaining my voice and the essential message. Thanks.

As I wrote this book I kept wondering, What if, at some point, one of my kids were to venture away from God into the "far country"? My biggest prayer for my sons (and any kids to follow) is that they will not just follow Christ but that they will follow him with passion and commitment. And if for some reason they do turn away, may God use this book—and more important, his Book—to bring them back.

LOOKING FOR SOMETHING MORE

Darius and I were having dinner and talking about our spiritual journeys.[1] As I was finishing my salad, he pointed to the Bible I had brought along.

"I no longer believe what my parents believe about that book," he said. His comment didn't surprise me. Darius's parents had called the week before, begging me—the new young-adults pastor—to do something with their "wayward" son. They feared that Darius had gone off the deep end with all of his questions. He was even investigating different religions—a fact his parents had mentioned to me with some degree of shame.

"I don't believe the Bible has all the answers," Darius told me. "I think there is value in other religions and other beliefs. I go to the mosque occasionally. And I've even tried the Mormon Temple. It's a mistake to settle on one thing too soon and then tell everyone else you've found the answer. It's better to expose yourself to different beliefs and different ways of life. You know what I'm saying?"

Darius's feelings are representative of a lot of the people I talk to. He questioned the notion of absolute truth and didn't appreciate the arrogance he perceived in Christianity's claim that Jesus is the only way to

God. As we dug into the main course, Darius put the ball back in my court. "So what do you think of all this?" he asked.

"Seems like you've got it all figured out," I said, smiling. "So I'm wondering if I should pay for this meal out of my own money or take it out of my expense account through the church."

"I'll pick up the tab," he said. "After all, I asked you to meet me for dinner."

"But why did you want to get together?" I asked. "Where does the conversation go from here? I've heard your story and all the twists and turns you've taken on your spiritual journey. You seem pretty set in what you believe about the failings of Christianity. Did you invite me to dinner so I could hear your journey? Or maybe to let me know that you're no longer under the control of your folks, that you've rejected their beliefs about the Bible?"

He chuckled and said, "Oh, you've talked to my parents. Let me guess; they gave you the save-our-boy speech?"

"Close to it. They aren't the first parents to use that speech, and they won't be the last. It's the part of my job as a minister that kind of ticks me off."

"Why does it bother you so much?" he asked.

"When I get the phone calls with the save-our-boy speech, it can come off like 'We messed him up, now *you* do something to fix him.' Like I'm supposed to take care of all the spiritual stuff during one dinner conversation."

"Well, I wouldn't say my parents messed me up," Darius said. "I'm twenty-nine, and they're not to blame for the choices I've made. But I'd be lying if I said they haven't influenced some of my current beliefs—especially my views of religious faith and the Bible."

I probed a little more into how Darius had developed his views on Scripture. And that's when he really began to talk.

"I grew up in the church. Some people referred to me and my siblings as 'church bums.' You know, the kind of people who are always there whenever the doors of the church are open. The only way we could get out of going to church was the same way we got out of school: We had to be running a temperature. No excuse like 'My stomach hurts' or 'I've got a sore throat' would fly. It had to be something verifiable.

"And you couldn't wear just any old thing to church. You had to dress up. Why? 'Because God gave his best for us,' my mother would say. For the longest time I actually thought that was a verse in the Bible. I was shocked when I went to church a few years ago with some white friends and saw people wearing shorts and T-shirts. I just knew that God Almighty was going to put a curse on them or something. Anyway, when I was growing up, proper dress was a must: shoes shined, clothes pressed, and hair neatly in place.

"When we got to church, the adults would go to their Sunday school, and the kids would go off to their own classes. When that was over we had to sit in the sanctuary for the service. Let's just say this was not my favorite event of the week. For starters, it was long. It would begin at eleven a.m. and would go sometimes until almost two in the afternoon. I couldn't stand the music, and I hated the sermons.

"Our pastor was a huge man who loved to scream and wail. He would carry on for anywhere from forty-five minutes to an hour and some change. This scared the mess out of me. He came across like he would rip your heart out if you did anything wrong. I guess that's why we kids avoided him. Even when we got a little older and started making fun of church people—especially how they would dance and shout—we would never make fun of our pastor. That was just too scary.

"The older I got, the less I liked him. I got past his screaming and wailing, but what really bothered me were some of his beliefs that I didn't agree with. For instance, my mother was involved in helping with the high-school ministry. When no one else would volunteer, she could be counted on to teach the class and take us on special trips. Well, one day that all ended because the pastor told her the Bible says it's improper for a woman to lead young men. I can still see my mother crying in the parking lot after she got that news.

"And his comments on rap music sent me over the edge. Back then rap was a new thing that all of us kids loved. We would stay up late on Friday nights listening to Doug E. Fresh, Dana Dane, and Run-D.M.C. on the radio. We even tried to be rappers, forming our own groups and sneaking to the church bathroom on the break between Sunday school and the worship service. There, behind closed doors, we'd battle against each other to see who was the best. I can still hear the fearful voice of one of my friends: 'Keep it down! They're gonna hear us!'

"One time my parents decided to throw a party with a prom theme to celebrate their sixteenth wedding anniversary. This was when rap was really starting to catch on. Someone said they'd never heard it before, and they wanted to hear some. Everyone looked at me, so I ran off to get some music. When I popped in the tape and pushed the button, the Beastie Boys' 'License to Ill' blared out. The look on my ultraconservative parents' faces—as they and their friends listened to the vulgarity coming from three white rappers—was priceless! Then all I could hear was 'Turn that off *now!*' I must have been grounded for two weeks. But it was worth it.

"Then there was all the stuff from my pastor. My friends were really good at rap, and they were also starting to get on fire for God. So they decided to rap about God. One night at a church concert, these three guys got up and started rapping about God, and the people really seemed to be into it. The song finished, and the pastor got up. Before he even opened his mouth, I knew there was going to be trouble, because he had this look of wrath. I don't remember everything he said, but the gist of it was, 'You can't follow God and listen to rap music.' As he condemned the music, he pointed at the Bible, as if to say, 'What I'm saying is right here in this book.' We were devastated."

Now Darius had my attention. "What happened to the kids in the rap group?" I asked.

"They eventually left the church, and two of them never made it back. Who can blame them? They…we…were given a picture of what the Bible was about, and none of us wanted it. The only reason I didn't leave was because I couldn't. I was still living at home. But you know what's interesting? My parents never admitted that what the pastor said was wrong. I guess that's because in my home you never spoke against the pastor, no matter what he did or said.

"Or maybe they actually agreed with him. Their beliefs weren't that different from his. They came across like the Bible said you couldn't wear earrings or have a tattoo. My cousin recently got her tongue pierced, and to hear my parents talk, you would have thought she was going straight to hell.

"They live in a black-and-white world. There's one list of what's good and another list of what's bad. The Bible was always presented as a list of dos and don'ts, a big spoiler of good times. You can't have sex. You can't drink. You can't smoke. You can't rap. You can't, you can't, you can't! That's the home and the church I grew up in. So when I went to college and discovered that no one cared what I did, the first thing I did was ditch the church. Since no one was looking over my shoulder, I felt free to drink, smoke, and spend the night at my girlfriend's. I felt liberated, and I never looked back."

Darius's experiences had profoundly shaped his views on the Bible and Christianity, and at age twenty-nine, he was still looking for a religion that made sense to him. He viewed the Bible as an archaic, judgmental book that didn't have much to do with real life. Darius was enjoying his freedom, and getting him to a place where he might give Scripture a closer look seemed unlikely. Given his negative church experience, I was still wondering why he had invited me to dinner.

"I can see you've been burned by the church," I said. "So why did you want to meet with me?"

He paused for a few seconds. "I guess I've got a lot of anger. I've often felt like I should sue my parents and that pastor for brainwashing me. I don't agree with their beliefs, but when I check out any other religion, it still feels like that's not exactly 'it.'

"It's like this. You know how you wake up one day and say, 'I need a new shirt,' but you don't really know the exact kind of shirt you're looking for? You go to the mall and try on a couple. They're really nice, but you don't buy them because you sense that these particular shirts are just not 'it.' And then you go to one last store, you see a shirt, and your brain clicks—'That's it!'

"That's how it's been with me. I go to the mosque, and I occasionally have coffee with some elders from the Mormon church. But my brain hasn't clicked and said, 'That's it!' I've also thought a lot about Christianity and the Bible, but I don't think that's 'it' either."

I wondered if Darius realized that the religion he was sold when he was growing up was an imposter, a distortion of God and his story. I asked him if he'd be willing to explore a different take on the Bible—one that was drastically different from what he'd known as a kid. He shrugged his shoulders as if to say, "Sure, I'll listen to what you have to say."

He paid the bill, and we left the restaurant for a coffee shop a few blocks away.

DADDY

A Love Story on a Grand Scale

> He didn't want us to call him Daddy. I wanted to call him
> Daddy so bad.
>
> —Michael Jackson

> *Abba,* Father.
>
> —Paul the apostle (Galatians 4:6)

Darius and I were waiting for our drinks at the little café when we noticed Michael Jackson's picture on the television. The announcer was reporting yet another strange twist in the entertainer's life.

I asked Darius if he had watched the recent television documentary on Michael Jackson. He hadn't, but I admitted that I was one of the millions of Americans who tuned in that night. As Martin Bashir interviewed Jackson, I ran the gamut of emotions from disappointment to anger to embarrassment. (Yes, I'm a huge fan.) I was saddened as I watched the man who had changed so drastically from the little Michael that America had first come to know and love. The extent of this change was captured in the documentary as the interviewer and the singer sat in a theater in Jackson's home, watching old performances of Michael and his brothers. The Jackson Five were singing classic songs like "ABC" and

"I Want You Back." While the two men watched the films, the image on the TV screen toggled back and forth between the young Michael Jackson and the troubled adult who was watching the old films. He had not just matured; he had become a different person.

Bashir asked probing questions about Jackson's childhood, particularly his relationship with his father. In great pain Michael reflected on the beatings his father had given him and his brothers. Beatings for missing dance steps. Beatings for not singing the right note. Michael fought back tears as he recalled the times when he wanted so desperately to go across the street to play with the neighborhood kids. But his father forced him and his brothers to rehearse long hours in the studio while other kids played outside.

As Michael recalled his early childhood, he said he never referred to his father as Daddy, but always as Joseph. In a poignant statement, Michael revealed, "He didn't want us to call him Daddy. I wanted to call him Daddy so bad."[1]

That insight answered so many questions. Questions about the adult Michael's climbing trees at his Neverland Ranch. Questions about the amusement park he had built on his property. And even questions about his having children sleep over at his house and sometimes even in his bedroom—not that it justifies his actions. As a child, Michael's heart had desperately cried "Daddy," but his father never connected to his son's heart cry. And consequently, Michael never developed to the point of healthy maturity.

Even though Darius had not seen the Michael Jackson documentary, I thought it might be helpful to talk about the similarities between the cruel and unreasonable Joseph Jackson and the way many people view God as Heavenly Father.

"A lot of folks—Christians included—think of God as nothing more than a stern rule giver," I said to Darius. "And they understand the Bible to be a long list of commands, a discourse on correct behavior. Do this;

don't do that! Wear this; don't wear that! They don't read the Bible as the story of a loving relationship between God and the people whose hearts he is trying to win. Instead, they read the Bible and see something similar to what Michael Jackson saw in his father: a stern, unyielding drill sergeant.

"Now it's true that Joseph Jackson helped create the King of Pop and one of the best music groups of all time. But all this was at the expense of his relationship with Michael. Joseph created a son who is now unhealthy in a lot of ways. Sure, Michael can do all the right dance steps, but he doesn't have a close relationship with his father. And that's the way it is with many Christians. They can do all the required dance steps of the religious life, but when it comes to having an intimate relationship with God as their Father, it's just not there. They don't see the Bible telling a love story between them and God."

I suspected that this described Darius's religious background. It was likely he had always thought of God as a harsh dictator rather than a loving Father. So I ventured a guess.

"From what you've told me, this is like the religious teaching you received," I said. "The men at your church—especially the pastor—were nothing more than Joseph Jacksons who banged on the Bible and told you to do the right dance steps. They wanted you to look nice, but they didn't care about what was going on inside you. So you dressed up for church, kept quiet during the sermon, and recited your Easter speeches. But as you say, that wasn't 'it.' Somewhere along the line your heart was desperately longing for Daddy, and all you got was Joseph."

THE ESSENCE OF GOD'S NARRATIVE

As we think about God, we are brought to the core story that is told in the Bible. The core message is not about making sure you dress properly for church, stand up during the singing, and kneel when it's time for prayer. The essence of the Bible is the story of a Father who desperately wants to be involved with his creation.

God is not—as the deists portray him to be—some divine clock-maker who wound creation up, set the hands on the clock, and then removed himself from the scene. He is, and seeks to be, intimately and actively involved with his creation. In other words, God is immanent. But he is also transcendent—unique and sovereign—over his creation. As a popular Bible scholar has said, "The God of the Bible is no abstract deity removed from and uninterested in his creation. The Bible is the story of God's involvement with his creation, and particularly the people in it."[2]

God's activity among the people he created is a major theme that runs throughout the Bible. In the Old Testament we see him walking with Adam in the cool of the evening, visiting Abram at Haran, appearing to Moses in a burning bush, sleeping over with Daniel in a lonely lions' den, and speaking to his people countless times through his prophets.

Sadly, many have called the period of time between the Old Testament and the New Testament the four hundred silent years, suggesting that God wasn't involved in the world during that time. The perception is that God was taking a break to get things together for his biggest move. But nothing could be further from the truth. Those four hundred years were crucial in God's plan. During that time he raised up the Greeks who, through their conquering of the world, introduced a dominant language. Then he used the Romans to help simplify travel. Both the dominant language and the system of Roman roads were huge developments, instrumental to the establishment and advancement of God's kingdom on earth. Paul the apostle reflected on this when he said, "But when the time had fully come, God sent his Son, born of a woman, born under law."[3] God didn't take a vacation. He was actively involved with his creation, setting the stage for his greatest act of love.

If you question the reality of God's involvement in the world, think about the first four books of the New Testament. The story we read there has nothing to do with a distant heavenly being who watches things unfold on earth but does nothing about it. It's just the opposite. The high point of the Bible comes when "the Word became flesh and made his dwelling among us."[4] God was so consumed with love for his creation that he came to earth to live here. He wanted to hang with us so we could enjoy a relationship with him, having the same privilege Adam enjoyed—the privilege of *walking* with God.

The heart sigh of those who grasp God's extended hand and embrace his activity in their lives is "*Abba,* Father."[5] The word *Abba* comes from the Aramaic language, the language Jesus spoke. It's a term of endearment, the equivalent of a little girl sitting on her father's lap and sweetly calling, "Daddy." It's akin to a father coming home after a long day at work and being greeted by a child who runs to him with outstretched arms and gleefully exclaims, "Daddy!" Whenever a child says "Daddy," it's an invitation for the father to become actively involved in the child's life. It's a call for engagement and relationship.

It's the same with us as we feel a stirring of spiritual desire. Our hearts long to cry out, "*Abba,* Father." Our souls long to sigh "Daddy!" and to find that there really is a loving Father out there.

The Bible is best understood as the story of God and his dealings with humanity. The heartbeat of this narrative is an immanent God extending his hand to the people he created and inviting them to experience his work and activity in their lives. Some people take hold of his hand and experience the blessings of the journey with him. Others push his hand away and suffer the repercussions of rejecting his love.

David, the greatest king of ancient Israel, grabbed God's hand at an early age. He held tightly to God in the valleys of life when he was on the run from the murderous King Saul. In contrast, Saul pushed God's hand away and experienced the calamities that come from living life apart from

God. Satan shook Job with all his might, causing him to suffer almost every conceivable tragedy, but he couldn't shake Job loose from God. Amid great pain, Job still trusted God, saying, "In his hand is the life of every creature and the breath of all mankind."[6] The apostle Paul, who wrote much of the New Testament, had a firm grasp on Daddy's hand even when he faced ridicule from the intellectual elite of ancient Greece. In front of the philosophers and thinkers gathered on Mars Hill in Athens, Paul boldly proclaimed, "For in him [God] we live and move and have our being."[7]

Darius had been listening patiently to all this as he sipped his cappuccino.

"I agree that a story about a loving God who comes through for his people is appealing," he said, "but you've got to admit there's a lot in the Bible besides that."

"You're right," I said. "But for now we're talking about the Bible's core message. At its heart, the narrative of Scripture shows a Father with his hands outstretched to the people he created. Meanwhile, the people God created are portrayed in various stages along the journey with their Father. We read of times when the people are holding Daddy's hand tightly and other times when they choose to let go.

"Here's a good example. Jonah, the reluctant prophet, demonstrates the tension of holding on and letting go. God tells him to go to the city of Nineveh, the most evil place on earth at that time, to warn the people of God's impending judgment. That sort of thing was Jonah's job, since he was a prophet. But instead of obeying, Jonah decides to take the next ship going in the opposite direction. Because of his disobedience, Jonah is eventually thrown overboard and is swallowed by a giant fish. While he's inside the belly of the whale, God gets Jonah's attention and begins to turn his heart. Finally, Jonah surrenders to Daddy, goes to Nineveh, and sees a great revival take place.

"The Jonah narrative shows us a patient, gracious God who extends his hand to us even when we are least deserving of his mercy.[8] Even when we are deliberately heading in the opposite direction. Even when we thumb our noses at God and tell him he's irrelevant, nonexistent, too narrow, too harsh, and entirely not to our liking. Even then, he still extends his hand to us.

"When we grab hold of God's hand, we experience great blessings—though it doesn't mean we no longer encounter difficulties in life. But when we let go of God, we find ourselves in bondage because of our disobedience. In the Old Testament, whenever the people of Israel let go of God's hand and decided to fend for themselves, they ended up being carried off into slavery in some foreign country. Yet the one constant theme of God's narrative is a patient Father with outstretched arms, waiting for his children to come home and cry, 'Daddy.'

"Darius, the Bible isn't primarily about laying down the law and making sure nobody has any fun. It's a story about a relationship of love that takes the form of a journey through life. It's God reaching out to the people he created, and their response to his love. While some people never come to God, and all of us leave his side from time to time to try things on our own, the narrative points to a patient Father who does everything he can to give everyone an opportunity to experience his work and his presence in their lives. This is the narrative of Scripture, and it's the same narrative that is told in countless lives of people who populate the planet today.

"And here's one more thing to think about: This is no ordinary story. It's authentic. Real. Even sacred."

chapter two

THE SACRED NARRATIVE

Pay Close Attention to the God Encounters

Yet surely in the presence of Your life-giving Godhead no
unbecoming thought should arise and no creature possess my
heart, for I am about to receive as my guest, not an angel, but
the very Lord of angels.

—Thomas à Kempis, *The Imitation of Christ*

Holy, holy, holy is the LORD Almighty;
the whole earth is full of his glory.

—Isaiah the prophet (Isaiah 6:3)

A
s Darius and I finished our cappuccinos, our conversation turned
to heroes. You never know who a person's hero will be. Often it's
a teacher or a coach. Sometimes it's a parent or a grandparent. For Darius, it was a prizefighter. One of the greatest of all time: Muhammad Ali.

"I grew up in the South, just like Ali," Darius said. "Like him I encountered the limitations that society tried to force on me just because I
wasn't white. But Ali proved that limitations have power only if you allow
yourself to be limited. You don't have to cave in to the man. You can
choose to live your own life. That's a big reason why I look up to Ali."

I knew what Darius meant. Ali remains an inspiration to millions of people, and not just African Americans. Ali's story is like oxygen, especially for those who feel the cards are stacked against them.

Darius knew many of the details of Ali's childhood, but he had never heard the story about the young Cassius Clay on the day his bicycle was stolen. It's a story worth retelling, so I did.

The air was crisp as the two boys hopped on their bicycles and headed off to the Louisville Home Show, an annual event where African Americans could learn about businesses that provided services in their community. The boys spent the day canvassing the floor of Columbia Auditorium, taking in the sights as they made their way from one booth to the next. They enjoyed popcorn, cotton candy, and other unhealthy snacks their parents frowned upon. Then, like all great days, this one had to end.

As the boys walked outside to begin the journey home, they were shocked to find that one of their bikes was missing. The boy whose bicycle had been stolen began crying. When an elderly woman asked what was wrong, the upset boy explained what had happened. The woman suggested that he talk to the police officer stationed in the auditorium. She told the boys they could fill out a report—perhaps the police would find the bicycle. The two boys ran back inside the auditorium.

When the police officer asked what was wrong, one boy said, "Mister, someone stole my bike, and when I find him I'm going to whup his butt." The cop told the boy that if he was going to fight, he should get some training, and that he would be honored to train the young boy.

The police officer was a part-time boxing trainer named Joe Martin. And the twelve-year-old boy was, of course, Cassius Clay. This encounter between a devastated boy and a police officer who was moonlighting as a trainer would have worldwide ramifications. The young Cassius Clay was transformed from a scared twelve-year-old to the eventual heavyweight champion of the world. He would fulfill his own prophecy as "the greatest of all time."[1]

As a hero to millions, Ali was bigger than life. But the hero who changed the fighter's life forever was an ordinary police officer. As I looked across the booth at Darius, I reminded him, "Never underestimate the power of life's 'little' encounters."

Lives have been rerouted and radically changed because of a single unexpected encounter. Career paths have been altered, businesses have been started, and leaders have taken their first step toward greatness because of a seemingly minor encounter. And if human encounters produce such revolutionary changes, consider the potential outcome of the unexpected encounters that take place between humanity and God. Those are the encounters that make up the heart of the Bible. Such encounters have implications not only for this life but also for eternity.

Cassius Clay converted to Islam as an adult and changed his name to Muhammad Ali. For all the differences between Islam, Judaism, and Christianity, there is one historical figure who is honored by all three religions: Abraham. Abraham began life with the name of Abram. He was minding his own business in a place called Haran when God entered the picture. There is no indication in the Bible that Abram had been praying for help or that he had asked God to intervene in his life. In fact, Abram was a landowner and a successful businessman, a man who was enjoying the good life.

God showed up anyway. He told Abram that he had decided to bless anyone who blessed Abram and to curse those who cursed Abram. Not only that, but God promised to bless *every nation on earth* through Abram.[2] When God got hold of Abram, he not only changed his name to Abraham, but he radically changed Abraham's life.

Abraham and his wife, Sarah, had no children. But God promised that they'd have a son in their old age. Even though Sarah was well beyond childbearing years, God enabled her to become pregnant, and she gave birth to Isaac, the son of promise. This was the son who would carry on the family line. Isaac married Rebecca, and they had twin sons, Esau and Jacob.

From the start Jacob was trouble. He lied and manipulated, stealing his twin brother's birthright. He even lied to his dying father so he could rob the blessing that rightfully belonged to Esau. Nothing was beneath Jacob. Then one day God showed up. He met Jacob at a place called Peniel, where he not only changed Jacob's name to Israel, but he changed Jacob's character as well. Jacob was changed because of a God encounter.

God continued to interrupt the affairs of his people over the centuries that followed. Jacob's son Joseph became prime minister of Egypt, and all of Jacob's family later moved to Egypt to survive a famine. After Joseph's death, the Hebrews became slaves in Egypt, where they grew into a great nation. Then Moses encountered God in a burning bush, and God commissioned him to lead the people from bondage in Egypt to the Promised Land in Canaan. Moses liberated them from slavery, but the history of Israel continued to be one of wandering, finally finding a home, then being taken into exile, and then returning to the land God had given them. Throughout centuries of strength and weakness, times of secure borders followed by foreign occupation, they continued to have encounters with God.

Then, two thousand years ago in an unlikely backwater town, came the pivotal God encounter of all time. An unknown Jewish teenager named Mary, from the village of Nazareth, received word from God that she had been chosen to help fulfill the promise that God had given to Abraham. This was the central prophecy and greatest hope of the Jewish religion: the promise of a Messiah.

Mary was probably no older than thirteen on the day God showed up. She wasn't from a wealthy family; she had no access to the channels of religious or political influence. In fact, people often dismissed her hometown with the question, "Can anything good come from there?"[3]

God often shows up in the most unlikely places and appears to the most unlikely people. In this case, God sent an angel to tell Mary that she would be the one who would give birth to the Messiah, the promised Savior of Israel. Needless to say, Mary's life was forever changed by this encounter with the Almighty.

The sacred narrative is filled with examples of men and women whose lives were transformed because of an encounter with God. The intersection of the divine with the human is a major theme of Scripture. Again and again, the story records a collision of the secular with the sacred. God keeps dropping by to interrupt his creation. These encounters between God and humanity are far from being ordinary or normal. They occur so frequently, in fact, that they aren't the exception; they're the rule.

Darius turned out to be a great listener, but I was wondering what he thought about all this. Our conversation returned to earthly heroes and specifically to Muhammad Ali.

"What makes the encounters between Abraham and God, or Jacob and God, or Moses and God different from that encounter between the young Cassius Clay and a police officer named Joe Martin?" I asked.

"Well," Darius said, "based on what you've been saying, every one of those encounters changed somebody. Ali started down the long road to world heavyweight champion after he met the cop who agreed to teach him to box."

"In every instance, a life was changed dramatically," I said. "But in the case of Abraham or Jacob or Moses—and many others like them—the encounter was with no mere mortal. They were approached by God, the Creator of the universe, a Being who can be compared to no other.

"It's hard to describe how 'otherly' God is. But maybe that's the point. God is unlike anything else we've ever experienced and anyone else we've ever known. No words or ideas really capture God's 'otherliness.' The Bible sometimes uses the word *awesome* to describe God. But in our world it describes hamburgers, experiences, and fast cars, so *awesome* doesn't pack the required punch. Even if we said that God is *indescribable*, that wouldn't convey how unique he is. We've all experienced things we'd call indescribable. Gazing at Niagara Falls. Peering into the Grand Canyon. Or maybe even hearing our favorite singer perform live. Those experiences are difficult to put into words. Yet they're all natural, earthly things."

"So what's the word?" Darius asked. "If God wants to cross our path and show us he's interested in us, there has to be a way to talk about God. There has to be some word that describes him. What is it?"

"The one word that captures God and his unique nature is the word *holy*," I said. "What makes encountering God so different from encountering your favorite professional athlete or the president of the United States? It's that God is holy, and no one in his creation is."

THE BIG DEAL ABOUT HOLINESS

In the Old Testament book of Isaiah, the kingdom of Israel has split into two sometimes-warring nations: Israel and Judah. The nation of Judah is in a state of crisis because its king has died. The capable ruler and king, Uzziah, is gone, and Isaiah the prophet is reeling from the loss. With Uzziah in charge, Isaiah could move freely throughout the palace, since Uzziah leaned heavily on Isaiah for guidance. Now, with the king dead, God seizes the moment to reveal himself to Isaiah as he never has before.

In great detail, the prophet describes his encounter with God. The essence of God's nature is summed up in the words of the seraphs that Isaiah hears. They call out in praise to God: "Holy, holy, holy is the LORD Almighty; the whole earth is full of his glory."[4] When Isaiah's path intersects with God's, he doesn't just encounter God. He encounters a *holy* God!

I might have gotten a little too animated as I was talking, because Darius looked around to see if anyone in the café was staring at us.

"Yeah, God's holy," he said. "We all know that. So what's the big deal?"

"I know this isn't new to you," I said. "We've both heard it hundreds if not thousands of times at church. But if you're like me, you've heard God's holiness described but not really defined.

"For example, when I was a teenager, I was always hearing the word *holiness* in connection with not having sex. Then when I went off to a strict Bible college, holiness was associated with not going to movies and not drinking. All the while I was missing out on exactly what it meant to be holy."

"Well, what is it then if it's not a limitation on your life, like not having sex with your girlfriend or not running around and drinking?" Darius asked.

"When we talk about the holiness of God, we're talking about *his absolute intrinsic and ethical purity*. God is completely pure in who he is and what he does. One leading theologian calls this God's "transcendent holiness." Because of his absolute purity, God is *set apart* from the rest of his creation.[5] Remember, God is entirely 'other,' unlike anything he created."

"Purity, holiness, entirely 'other,'" Darius said. "What are you trying to get at?"

"God's holiness is a big deal because of the way Isaiah describes his God encounter," I said. "When Isaiah crosses paths with God, three times the seraphs say that God is holy. *Three times.* Often in the narrative of Scripture, things are repeated to get our attention. For example, when Jesus really wanted his audience to catch a point he was about to make, he'd begin by saying 'truly, truly.'[6] It was his way of saying, 'Now listen up so you won't miss this point.'

"And while such repetition was common, very rarely do we see something declared *three* consecutive times," I continued. "In fact, this is the *only* aspect of God's nature that is stated three times in a row in Scripture. Why? Because all of God's other attributes and actions flow from his holiness. Nothing else about God would be godlike without his holiness.

"Now here's where the narrative of Scripture becomes sacred. A completely holy God, who is absolutely pure in who he is and what he does, decides to encounter sinful, stained, unholy humanity. Both of us, Darius, plus everyone we know, are marked by sin. David, the greatest earthly king of Israel, when he reflected on his adultery with a married woman named Bathsheba, cried out, 'Surely I was sinful at birth, sinful from the time my mother conceived me.'[7] The apostle Paul declared, 'For all have sinned and fall short of the glory of God.'[8] He also quoted from the Old Testament: 'There is no one righteous, not even one; there is no one who understands, no one who seeks God. All have turned away, they have together become worthless; there is no one who does good, not even one.'"[9]

"This is nothing new," Darius said. "I grew up in church, and believe me, the one message they drove home every chance they got was how sinful I was."

"I'm not judging you," I said. "We're in this together. In God's eyes we're dirty, filthy people whose hearts and actions are wicked. We're the exact opposite of a holy God. We're the opposite of what God is. And yet this holy, sacred God chooses to extend his hand and become actively involved in our lives. It's pretty amazing stuff."

THE ENCOUNTER THAT CHANGES PEOPLE

If you read the Bible, you see God choosing to get close to some really dirty people. Just for starters, God encountered:

- Abraham, who was a liar. He denied that Sarah was his wife just to make things easier for himself when he got into a jam. Abraham's lie endangered Sarah, but God protected her.

- Moses, who was a murderer. Before he freed the Hebrews from slavery, he killed an Egyptian.
- Rahab, who was a whore. When Hebrew spies came to scout out Rahab's city, Jericho, she sheltered them. God honored her actions, and she wound up being an ancestor of Jesus.
- David, who, like Moses, was a murderer. He killed to try to cover up his adultery with Bathsheba, the wife of Uriah the Hittite.
- Jonah, a bitter, rebellious man who ran when God told him to warn the people of Nineveh about God's coming judgment. Not only that, when God spared the city after the people turned away from their sin, Jonah threw a temper tantrum because God didn't do what Jonah wanted him to do.
- Peter, a coward who denied Jesus when the chips were down.
- Paul, a persecutor and murderer of Christians. In fact, he was on his way to persecute followers of Jesus in another city when God met him in a blinding light.

These people had two things in common. First, they were dirty people, and second, they met God. And because of the collision between dirty humanity and a pure God, their lives were transformed forever.

This is the heartbeat of the sacred narrative: a holy God interrupts the affairs of sinful humanity and changes our lives forever. This is what makes the story sacred. To think that God in his holiness would want to be intimately involved in my life is beyond anything I could ever comprehend. This isn't just for people who lived thousands of years ago. God has continued to cross paths with people throughout history.

John Newton was a wealthy man who made his fortune off the slave trade. He sailed to the western shores of Africa, packed people onto ships, and took them to America. There, on the auction block, they were poked and prodded and sold to the highest bidder. Family members would be separated and would likely never see each other again, thanks in part to this evil man.

Countless times he made the ocean journey. Then on a trip back to Europe from America, Newton was thumbing through a book called *The Imitation of Christ*. As he read the words of Thomas à Kempis, God's Spirit began to move in the heart of the slave trader. The holy God encountered this sinful man. Newton surrendered his life completely to the Lord, and after several years of struggle, finally broke free from the lucrative business of slave trading to enter the ministry.

In later years Newton experienced bouts of guilt as he reflected on the horrible things he had done. He couldn't understand why this holy God would encounter him, an evil man who had done so much harm to so many innocent people. Finally, it clicked. In a moment of enlightenment he wrote these words:

> Amazing grace! how sweet the sound,
> That saved a wretch like me!
> I once was lost, but now am found;
> Was blind, but now I see.[10]

These words are sung today in countless churches and even at many secular events. The song is also sung by folk singers and pop singers and gospel groups. It is probably the best-known hymn in the English language.

John Newton is yet another example of a sinful person whose path intersected with a holy God. That's the core message of the sacred narrative—a narrative that is not only sacred, it's alive. And it continues to redirect the lives of those who have God encounters today.

WHY ME?

The Collision of the Divine with the Depraved

I stared at the great man who had taken the time to write to me
when I was a convict…pausing for breath, he called my name.
It was like an electrical shock.

—MALCOLM X, *The Autobiography of Malcolm X*

What is man that you are mindful of him?

—DAVID, KING OF ISRAEL (Psalm 8:4)

D arius set his coffee cup down and looked at me. "You know, the
way you refer to the Bible as a sacred narrative opens a whole
new way for me to think about the Bible. I guess I'm like most people;
I'm naturally drawn to stories. It's like giving me a window to see the
meaning, to really catch the point. You know what I mean?"

"Sure," I said. "As you've probably picked up by now, I find myself
drawn to stories as well. It's how I see things. And when you think about
it, our love for stories is hardly anything new. Jesus did much of his teaching through stories, and they were usually simple stories that his agrarian
audience could understand. He talked about things like mustard seeds
and plowing and planting. These kinds of stories allowed people to understand and feel what he was talking about."

Darius seemed to have new interest in our conversation. "When I was in college," he said, "I went to a church with a friend of mine, and the pastor did something I thought was weird. Actually, I thought it was wrong. He was talking about legalism, and he showed a scene from *Les Misérables*. I go to movies all the time, but this was in church! In my upbringing, going to movies was frowned on. My pastor would never have dreamed of showing a movie clip during his sermon, even if it would have helped people understand what he was preaching about."

"So what did you think?"

"It was one of the most powerful sermons I've ever heard," Darius admitted. "It really got me thinking... Anyway, you were saying that Jesus used relevant stories so his audience could understand what he was saying. Well, I really think if he were here today, he'd refer to scenes from movies and even show some clips to illustrate his points."

"I agree. Movies are a powerful way to tell stories. With dramatic big-screen images, and dialogue and music amplified by surround sound, the stories that movies tell stay with us. They shape us and often change the way we think."

Since we were talking about movies, I asked Darius what he thought of Denzel Washington, one of my favorite actors.

"He's one of the best," Darius said. "In fact, he was so good in *Malcolm X* that I forgot he was an actor playing a part. Every time I watch that movie, Denzel *becomes* Malcolm!"

Darius was right. Washington's portrayal of the civil-rights leader was masterful. But he had far more going for him than great acting talent. He had the power of a great story in his favor.

Before he was an electrifying public speaker, Malcolm X was a two-bit hustler known as Red. He wore the finest clothes and drove the nicest cars. Yet his fashionable suits and expensive watches were only a facade to hide the emptiness in his heart as his life plummeted in a downward spiral of drugs, crime, and immorality. He was trapped, with no idea where to find deliverance.

According to Malcolm, deliverance came in a most unusual way. He was arrested on a burglary charge and sentenced to ten years in prison. While behind bars, Red was introduced to Islam and transformed into Malcolm X.

Like most new converts, his zeal for Islam knew no bounds. Every day he wrote to the Honorable Elijah Muhammad, head of the Black Muslims. He pored over the dictionary, stretching his mind to make up for the education he had lost due to a premature exit from school. And finally his prison time was up.

Soon after getting out, he went to hear Elijah Muhammad speak. Recalling the experience, Malcolm wrote:

> I stared at the great man who had taken the time to write to me when I was a convict.… [He] had spent years of his life in suffering and sacrifice to lead us, the black people, because he loved us so much. And then, hearing his voice, I sat leaning forward, riveted upon his words.[1]

As Malcolm listened, Muhammad stopped his message and called Malcolm's name. Malcolm reflected, "It was like an electrical shock. Not looking at me directly, he asked me to stand."[2]

Spike Lee, trying to capture the drama of this moment in a movie, set the first meeting between the two men in Elijah Muhammad's office. There, with tears and great timidity, Malcolm ascends the stairs and enters the presence of his hero, Elijah Muhammad. He quietly weeps as the messenger applies the story of Job to his life.[3]

While Spike Lee takes a bit of license in his version, he captures the essence of the actual event—Malcolm is in awe. His awe stems from the fact that such a great man would accept and embrace an ex-hustler and former con. The prevailing question that must have been whirling in his mind was "Why me?"

If the central message of the sacred narrative is God's interaction with humanity—the collision of the divine with the depraved—then the logical question that must follow is "Why?" Why would a holy God stoop so low to extend his hand to dirty, stained humanity?

Why would God grant astounding wisdom to a womanizer and idol worshiper named Solomon? Why would God endure for so long the faithless nation of Israel, the very people he had freed from slavery? Why would he put up with the bitter prophet Jonah, who ran away from God to avoid the mission he had been given? And why would God bother with a ruthless slave trader named John Newton?

WHY A MURDERER?

Moses's life in Pharaoh's palace is a distant memory, almost a forgotten episode as he treks across the dusty plains of Midian. No more being waited on or going to the finest schools in Egypt. He is now tending sheep. He used to peer out of the palace and watch his Hebrew brothers slaving away in the scorching sun as they struggled to build the pyramids of Egypt while he had grapes dropped in his mouth and felt the cool breeze of waving fans. Now look who's baking in the sun. Moses is in his fortieth year of being a shepherd. Soon he will die, and his son Gershom will take over the family business.

It's another hot day, and a brush fire is burning not too far from where Moses's sheep are grazing. He prepares to move the sheep, but there is one burning bush that causes him to stop and take a closer look. The bush is on fire, but it's not burning up. Moses wipes his eighty-year-old eyes with the back of his hand and looks again. Once again he sees a burning bush that is not being consumed by the fire.

Now God has Moses's attention.

God seizes the moment to redirect Moses's life. He figures Moses has spent enough time getting the training he needs to lead a vagabond nation referred to by the Egyptians as the "dusty ones." God speaks to Moses from inside the bush, instructing him to return to Egypt and tell Pharaoh, his former palace partner, to let God's people go. Sounds great, right? The sacred God commissioning an obscure shepherd to lead his people?

Moses has a ton of questions. He questions his own credibility, his eloquence (or lack thereof), and his credentials. At the heart of his questions is one big burning one: "Why me?" For the life of Moses, he can't figure out why this big, holy God would take the time to show up on the backside of a mountain to tell him that he's been chosen to lead God's people from bondage to freedom.

I'm sure the "why me?" questions didn't stop that afternoon. He undoubtedly asked "Why me?" again as he led the people out of Egypt and stretched his worn hands out toward a colossal sea, with the sound of Egypt's army rapidly approaching from behind. Later when God called Moses from the foot of Mount Sinai to commune with him as God inscribed the law on stone tablets, the single question "Why me?" was likely booming in the back of Moses' mind. And as he sat anxiously in the cleft of the rock, gazing at God's back, he had to have asked over and over again, "Why me? Wasn't I tending sheep not long ago, staring blankly at the lowered heads of God's dumbest creatures? And now I'm looking at something no man has ever lived to tell about! Why me?"[4]

That question keeps rolling on throughout the sacred narrative…

WHY A PROSTITUTE?

Rahab, a woman who lives in ancient Jericho, isn't the kind of person you'd bring home to meet your mother. Her list of lovers is long. There is no such thing as a man coming to her home just to hang out, except on this one occasion.

She hears a knock on her door. She checks her appointment book, assuming that she has a client scheduled that she's forgotten about. But there's nothing on the schedule. *Oh well,* she thinks as she quickly brushes her hair and washes her face. Standing outside are two men who definitely don't live on her side of the tracks. The sight of these men makes her smile. Could it be she's become so well known that her client base is extending as far as other countries?

She opens the door not knowing that her life is about to take a drastic turn. The men offer a quick greeting. They seem hurried and nervous, as if they're being followed. It quickly becomes clear that sex is the last thing on their minds.

Only a few minutes go by before there's a pounding on the door. Rahab excuses herself from her nervous guests so she can peer through the peephole. Outside are several agitated men from Jericho, and their clothes indicate they are messengers from the king. Her luck seems to be changing. Here are some wealthy clients. But then she puts two and two together: Two nervous Israelites are in her room, and several of the king's messengers have suddenly appeared at the door.

"Just a minute!" she cries to the men waiting outside. She turns and points to the roof, signaling for her guests to hide. She then slips on a robe to make it seem as if she's retired for the evening. The men outside resume their pounding.

Rahab addresses the king's messengers with a mixture of the truth and some deception. "Yeah, those spies were here, but I have no idea where they are now. I told them to take off, and where they went is anybody's guess."

The messengers look around just to make sure she isn't lying, and then they take off to hunt for the spies. Rahab sits down to calm her nerves before she goes to talk to the foreigners. As they chat she learns that her well-fortified city is about to be destroyed. She has serious reservations about what she's hearing. Could mighty Jericho really fall to this tiny nation? It's highly unlikely. But something inside makes her believe the men.

Several weeks later the walls fall. Rahab watches as neighbors are killed, former clients are slaughtered, and screaming women are captured. She feels a gentle hand on her shoulder. "It's okay," the man says as he leads Rahab and her family to safety.

The crumbled walls of Jericho are barely visible now. Rahab is filled with conflicting emotions as she struggles to keep up with the running Israelites. She's sad that her girlfriends are dead. Sad that her home and all her mementos are ruined. But she's grateful that she and her family were spared. And one burning question keeps rolling over in her mind: "Why me?"[5]

I wonder what's going through Rahab's mind today as she sits in heaven at the Savior's feet. Does she fully understand why God chose her, a prostitute, to shelter his spies? But that episode is only a small part of Rahab's story. The former whore married a man named Salmon, and together they had a son named Boaz, who became the great-grandfather of King David. And it was from the royal line of David that Jesus Christ, the King of the Jews, came!

Rahab, a foreigner from enemy territory, made it into the great Hall of Faith recorded in the New Testament book of Hebrews.[6] A former whore who is the ancestor of the Messiah? "Why me?" she must wonder.

WHY A PERSECUTOR OF CHRISTIANS?

The "why me?" question burned in the heart of Paul, formerly known as Saul. As a zealous defender of Judaism, Saul had held the garments of those who stoned Stephen, a leader in the fledgling church in Jerusalem. Saul later hunted down the followers of the renegade rabbi named Jesus.

The images of stoned or crucified Christians probably never fully evaporated from his memory.

Not only does God choose unlikely people such as Saul, he also seems to encounter those people in unlikely places. Saul was on his way to Damascus to persecute more Christians when God showed up, stopping him dead in his tracks. After that experience, Saul's name was changed to Paul, and his life headed off in the opposite direction. No longer the hunter, he was now the hunted. No longer watching the scourgings of Jesus's followers, Paul was now the one with a cat-o'-nine-tails digging into his back. I wonder if he thought about Stephen as the whip struck his bare flesh.

Not once did Paul complain about being stoned, being scourged, or being shipwrecked. In fact, he rejoiced in suffering for preaching the message of Jesus. But he was still flabbergasted at the notion of God calling a former persecutor of his children to become the leading preacher of the gospel to the Gentiles of the first century. Whether Paul sat in jail or journeyed throughout the known world to found churches, the question kept coming up: "Why me?" He wasn't questioning why he had to suffer. He was asking, "Why would God allow me to have the privilege of serving him? Why would a holy God commune with me, a former persecutor of God's people?"

He never got past that question: "For I am the least of the apostles and do not even deserve to be called an apostle, because I persecuted the church of God."[7] "I am less than the least of all God's people."[8]

I'm sure the "why me?" question came to mind as Paul sat with the Greek intellectuals at the world-famous Areopagus in ancient Athens, debating the leading philosophers and proclaiming the truth of Jesus, whose followers he had helped persecute. The "why me?" question roared as he reasoned with the Corinthians about Jesus Christ and when he pronounced anathema on the Judaizers, who tried to force followers of Jesus to subscribe to the requirements of the Old Testament Jewish law.[9] Paul never quite got over the "why me" question.

Moses. Rahab. Paul. A murderer, a prostitute, and a persecutor. Three people who were minding their own business—tending sheep, turning tricks, and persecuting followers of Christ—when God showed up and redirected their lives. They never got over the "why me?" question because they never forgot where they came from. Like Malcolm X in awe of his Muslim mentor, these three "dusty" people were in awe of a holy God who would stoop so low as to use them.

NEVER FORGET

"Here you go again with the dusty people," Darius said. "Isn't anyone in the Bible clean?"

"Well, in God's eyes no one is clean apart from Christ," I said. "And it's important to remember our days as dusty people, because it helps us appreciate the power of our encounters with God."

"Wait a minute," Darius interrupted. "I remember from Sunday school that when you're 'saved,' Jesus removes your sins, so that all the things you've done are forgiven and forgotten. Are you telling me that all that has changed?"

"Our sins are forgiven," I said. "That much is clear in the Scriptures. But forgotten? I don't know about that one. When the Bible says that God no longer remembers our sins, it doesn't mean he forgets about them in a literal sense. It simply means that he doesn't hold our sins against us. Read through the Old Testament, and you see a God who constantly reminds the Israelites of the sins of their fathers and encourages them to remember the error of their own ways."

"So God wants us to beat ourselves up over stuff we did in the past, maybe even years and years ago?" Darius asked.

"He doesn't want us to beat ourselves up, but he does show us that remembering is healthy. Remembering keeps us humble. You know what's funny, Darius? Probably the greatest teacher on grace was the apostle Paul. And he considered himself to be one of the greatest sinners of all humanity. Ironic, isn't it? But the more I ponder that paradox, the more it makes sense. Paul's great teachings on grace, which have stirred centuries of debate and contemplative thought, did not spring from some great intellectual treatise. While his teachings were inspired by the Spirit of God, those words also came from a man who constantly remembered the darkness of his past juxtaposed against the light and freedom of God's grace! He never forgot where he came from and what God did for him."

Jesus once used a weeping prostitute as an object lesson on never forgetting our sins. He showed the arrogant Pharisees—the religious leaders of the day—that they struggled with convenient amnesia as it related to their own dustiness. Speaking of the repentant prostitute, Jesus said, "Her many sins have been forgiven—for she loved much. But he who has been forgiven little loves little."[10] The prostitute never forgot the sinfulness of her past. How could she forget when she remembered the forgiveness of Christ?

This is a powerful story, and it haunts me. The stark contrast between the pious Pharisees and the humble whore bothers me because I see myself as a Pharisee. I'm pointing the finger in arrogant condemnation of the town slut, even questioning the actions of Jesus in showing mercy on her.

Not long ago a member of our church community was sleeping with just about every woman who crossed his path. Obviously, his actions were causing great damage to others in the church. I found myself getting angrier with him by the moment, as person after person came to me exposing his deeds. I was angry in part because he had wounded me deeply—he was my friend. We had spent hours together praying, having fun, and engaging in deep discussions. And now he had become my mental focal point as I wrote out a hellfire-and-brimstone sermon I was going to preach. I had him in mind, and my tone was abrasive. The hair stood up on the back of my neck whenever I saw him. I was boiling. He should know better than this!

While I was going through all this, I sat out on my patio to read the Scriptures. I couldn't focus. My mind kept going back to this wolf who claimed to be a sheep while he was wreaking havoc in our church. I wrote in my journal, "Why am I so angry with him?" Immediately God reminded me of my not-so-chaste past. I remembered a time when I was the prostitute sitting at Jesus's feet, shedding tears over my own dusty life. In my anger over the man in my congregation, I had forgotten why I needed God's forgiveness in my own life. Yes, I had a responsibility to exercise church discipline in the current situation, but my posture had not been one of grace. It had been one of condemnation. Like the Pharisees, I had convenient amnesia. I had forgotten.

Don't be so quick to forget "from whence you came." As you remember, however, don't let it bury you in regret. Be sure to acknowledge your newness in Christ. But as you live in Christ, never forget. Remembering keeps us where the prostitute was—doubled over and repentant at the Savior's feet. If we forget, we take our place with the hypocritical Pharisees—standing in arrogant condemnation of those who remember their need for mercy.

Those who remember are those who revisit the question, "Why me?"

THE LITTLE PEOPLE

Even God Loves an Underdog

Heaven will be filled with five-year-olds.

—BRENNAN MANNING, *The Ragamuffin Gospel*

Where is the wise man? Where is the scholar? Where is the
philosopher of this age? Has not God made foolish the wisdom
of the world?

—PAUL THE APOSTLE (1 Corinthians 1:20)

D arius and I had been talking for quite a while, and seeing as we
both had business to attend to the next day, we decided to call it
a night. Plus I wanted to give him time to think about why a holy God
would stoop so low to extend his hand to a dusty, ungrateful mass of
humanity. We got out our PDAs and arranged to meet again in two
weeks, this time for breakfast.

I got to the diner a little early and spent some time reading the paper,
catching up on current events. Darius soon showed up wearing his gym
clothes, looking like he'd had an intense workout.

"Do you work out much?" I asked.

"Oh yeah, gotta stay fit for the ladies," he said. And then, eyeing my slightly protruding stomach, he said, "I guess once you get married that kind of stuff doesn't mean that much."

"If by 'stuff' you mean 'the ladies,' I'd have to agree," I said, laughing.

Just then our server showed up. Darius placed his order and then, looking at me, told the server, "My friend will take two scrambled egg whites and a side of wheat toast."

Smiling, the server asked me, "Any butter with that, sir?"

Darius said, "Absolutely not!"

"Well, there you have it," I said as we handed her our menus.

As she walked off, Darius said, "Keep hanging with me, and I'll get you into shape. You know, I kind of like this arrangement. You can school me on the Bible, and I can school you when it comes to your body."

"That'll work," I said.

Finally our food came, and as we dove in, we started talking about the most famous racehorse in American history.

In 1938 there was plenty of news to keep the American public occupied. There were the exploits of the New York Yankees, with superstar Lou Gehrig. There were the New Deal initiatives of Franklin D. Roosevelt. Overseas, there was Germany's annexation of Austria and a growing uneasiness over Adolf Hitler's ambitions. With a depression at home and the growing threat of war overseas, there was plenty to read about in the newspapers.

But even with all of that going on, the number one newsmaker in the country was a crooked-legged racehorse by the name of Seabiscuit.[1] That's right, it wasn't the Great Depression or the growing threat posed by Hitler's Nazi regime. It was a racehorse that stole the headlines and the hearts of a panicked people eager for some good news.

When Seabiscuit was born, he showed no signs of future greatness.

His handlers actually hid him in a back barn when potential buyers came to look at the new horses. And adding insult to injury, Seabiscuit was ornery. He ran when he felt like it and raised hell when he felt like it, which was frequently. His eventual trainer tried calming the horse by putting a goat in his stall. When a groom later checked on the stall mates, he found Seabiscuit "walking in circles, clutching the distraught goat in his teeth and shaking her back and forth. He heaved her over his half door and plopped her down in the barn aisle."[2]

Seabiscuit's accomplishments are even more astonishing when you consider the people who rode him: Red "Cougar" Pollard and George "Iceman" Woolf. By 1936 Pollard had garnered a reputation as one of the worst riders anywhere. Several times he almost died on the track after being thrown from horses and breaking bones in the process. He even lost the sight in his right eye, a secret he kept from everyone.

Woolf's story is equally unimpressive. Among his many setbacks, the most devastating was his type 1 diabetes. Still, Team Seabiscuit prevailed. Laura Hillenbrand writes:

> His appearances smashed attendance records at nearly every major track and drew two of the three largest throngs ever to see a horse race in the United States. In an era when the United States population was less than half its current size, seventy-eight thousand people witnessed his last race, a crowd comparable to those at today's Super Bowls. As many as forty thousand fans mobbed tracks just to watch his workouts.... He galloped over Manhattan on massive billboards and was featured week after week, year after year, in *Time, Life, Newsweek, Look, Pic,* and *The New Yorker.*[3]

An ornery, crooked-legged horse, a one-eyed jockey, and a diabetic. This was the team that stole the headlines. In a country that had found despair to be a familiar neighbor, Team Seabiscuit offered hope. They were what was right with America—"little people" overcoming great odds and winning! If the most unlikely of horses, a washed-up jockey named Red, and a diabetic could win, then anyone could pull through the Great Depression and the threats of the next "great war."

People have always reserved a special place in their hearts for the underdog. We still love looking at video images of a joyful U.S. hockey team leaping across the ice, celebrating their 1980 Olympic victory over the heavily favored Soviet team. Our affection for the little people had us cheering for an over-the-hill Muhammad Ali against the formidable George Foreman in the sweltering heat of Zaire. Boxing fans still talk about the 1974 Rumble in the Jungle. In the movies the underdog theme won *Rocky* an Oscar and kept us coming back to watch the further exploits of an Italian bum from the streets of Philly as he prevailed over powerhouses like Apollo Creed and Clubber Lang. We can't resist cheering for the underdog.

And why shouldn't we favor the underdog? The little-people motif has its roots in the sacred narrative. A teenage shepherd boy named David dispatches the mammoth giant, Goliath, with a slingshot. A lone prophet, Elijah, stands in opposition to what seems like the whole world on Mount Carmel. A small, "inarticulate" man (or so the Corinthians thought) named Paul takes the message of the gospel to the Gentiles. Yep, God takes great pleasure in siding with the little people.[4]

GOD'S OWN LITTLE PEOPLE

If there ever was a nation that constantly found itself on "the wrong side of the card" come fight night, it was Israel—God's chosen people. From the time God informed Abraham that his descendents would become a nation,[5] God planned to use the Hebrews as a conduit of blessing to the entire world. Israel's opponents were to stand dumbfounded as they watched this "weak" nation overcome and shine in the midst of great adversity.

Mighty Egypt, an unrivaled world power, achieved that status primarily on the backs of Hebrew slaves. The nation of Israel lived in captivity for more than four hundred years. When the Egyptians feared that the Hebrew population was growing too big, they simply killed all the male infants—except one.[6] For four hundred years the Hebrews suffered under the heavy hand of the Egyptians who reminded them of their place at the bottom of the food chain.

Then God showed up.

He sent an exiled Moses—who had spent the last forty years tending sheep—and his brother, Aaron (who was negotiated into the deal by Moses to be his spokesperson), to Pharaoh to boldly declare that Egypt the great should let little Israel go. And if they did not, they would face dire consequences. I can almost hear the mocking tone in Pharaoh's voice: "Let me get this straight. You want me, king of the world's greatest empire, to just let you walk out of here? And if I don't, I'm in big trouble?" Surely tears came streaming down his face as he had the biggest laugh of his life. And he responded by cracking the whip a little harder, requiring the slaves to gather their own straw while maintaining their production of bricks. But Pharaoh soon realized God wasn't joking.

In ten very strategic plagues, almighty God (known as *Elohim*) proved his might over the Egyptians and their gods. The Egyptians depended on the Nile River for their existence, so God turned it to blood. Fish died and a terrible stench arose. Pharaoh arrogantly shrugged his shoulders and kept the Hebrews in bondage.

Next came frogs, gnats, flies, a plague on livestock, boils, hail, locusts, darkness, and then the death of the firstborn male in every family in Egypt, except in the Hebrew households that put the blood of a lamb over their doorposts.[7] With each plague, save the last, Pharaoh reneged on his promise to free the enslaved nation of Israel. Why would mighty Egypt sacrifice all this free labor, especially when the Israelites had absolutely no political or military might?

But finally, overcome by the death of his firstborn child, Pharaoh pleaded with Moses to take his people and leave. They did leave, but then the king had a change of heart. He summoned his best generals, mobilized his army, and took off in hot pursuit of the Hebrews. The Egyptian army caught them in a perfect place for military conquest. Pinned against the Red Sea, Israel faced its first big test of faith.

Calmly following God's instructions, Moses stretched forth his hand. In it he held his old staff, the same one he had used to lead sheep for all those years in Midian—and the one he would now use to lead his new "flock," Israel. In response to Moses's outstretched arm, God parted the sea. The "little" people walked through on dry ground, while the "mighty" people—armed to the teeth and riding in the best chariots of Egypt—pursued the Hebrews and were drowned in the sea. I wonder what went through Pharaoh's mind as he desperately tried to reach the water's surface, his body convulsing one last time. Probably the same thing that went through George Foreman's mind as he lay on the canvas that hot evening in Kinshasa, Zaire, looking up at the victorious Muhammad Ali: "How in the world did this happen?"

Score another one for the little people...

It's more than ironic; it's eerie. Before the Israelites left Egypt and experienced the upset of upsets, God had told them to never forget what he was about to do. He knew they had a rough road ahead of them. Wilderness wanderings. The threat of the Amalekites. Jericho. Babylon. Hitler. They would constantly be in positions where the odds would be stacked against them. Yet whenever they confronted another Red Sea, they were to look back and remember that it was God who delivered them.

Remembering God and his faithfulness to save is the message of the Old Testament Law as well as the story of Israel. In the first five books of the Law known as the Torah (and it can be argued for the whole of Scripture as well), the recurring message that comes blasting out of God's mouth is this: "Trust me. Obey me." If Israel would trust God and obey him completely, they would enjoy God's blessings to the max. If not, they would experience unwelcome consequences. Sadly, tiny Israel kept forgetting what God had done, preferring instead to rely on its own abilities.

HUNTED BY A KING

Never was Israel's lack of reliance on God more apparent than when the people decided they needed a change in government. It was as if they woke up one morning and realized that every other nation but them had a king—and these other nations seemed to be doing pretty well. So if Israel was going to be on the cutting edge of things, they reasoned, then of course they needed a king of their own!

Israel already had a leader—the prophet Samuel, who had been appointed by God to guide the nation. Now it was clear the people wanted a different leader. Samuel must have wondered what he had done to deserve this. But God, in an amazing display of vulnerability, told Samuel that he, God himself, bore the brunt of the insult. Israel was not guilty of rejecting Samuel; they were guilty of rejecting God as their Ruler. They demanded a radical change in government from a theocracy to a monarchy. It was as if they were saying, "Get out of the way, God, and give us an earthly king!"[8]

So God gave them what they wanted. And who did they want? Not a little person. No, they wanted someone tall, dark, and handsome. Someone who was, as my grandmother used to say, "easy on the eyes." A good king had to be handsome, right? He had to walk into a room and by his very presence command respect. Couldn't be some "runt." No, he had to be physically impressive. And he had to come from good stock. In Jewish terminology that meant from the tribe of Benjamin. So the most logical choice was Saul, a Benjamite who became Israel's first king. Samuel the prophet took the high road, anointed Saul as king, and turned him loose to rule with his brand new scepter.

Like most new things, the marriage between Israel and Saul began well. It was a glorious honeymoon. Then things started to go wrong. Saul broke God's law by offering burnt offerings and fellowship offerings at Gilgal. Then he failed to annihilate the Amalekites as God commanded.[9] That was the last straw. God decided he had had enough. He told Samuel, "Let's get Israel another king, and let's do it my way."

This time the king would lack the glamour that had commended Saul in the eyes of the people. In fact, the second king of Israel was, literally, a "little person." Samuel took his oil and went to the home of Jesse, a man with eight sons. Jesse presented all but one of his sons to the prophet. Each son took his turn standing in front of Samuel, who was poised to let the oil drip on one of these handsome studs. But each time, God said, "No." What gives? Did the prophet show up at the wrong house? Finally, Samuel asked Jesse if he had any other sons. Surprised, Jesse said the only one left was his youngest boy, whom he didn't think stood a chance to make the cut. Instead of bringing him to the audition, Jesse had sent this son out to tend sheep.

Sweaty and out of breath, David hadn't had a chance to get cleaned up before presenting himself to the prophet. But from the moment Samuel saw him, he knew. God said, "He's the one." A little shepherd boy was anointed king as the sun began to set—and his life was about to take a drastic turn.[10]

The nation of Israel was at war with the Philistines. There in the valley stood the enemy giant, Goliath. If ever there was an intimidating sight, it was this fearsome giant. Born several millennia too soon, today Goliath would be a millionaire several times over, with young teenage boys paying top dollar to see his exploits on WWE SmackDown! But in his time, all he knew how to do was wage war and taunt the little people.

No one would stand up to him because in their eyes he was big and powerful, and they weren't.

Surveying the scene, David was incensed. Who would dare insult the armies of the living God? Luckily David was naive enough to believe that with God he could conquer this guy—a belief that invited plenty of laughter. The Israelites didn't want to send the shepherd boy against the giant without any protection, so they tried to put Saul's armor on him. Again, laughter exploded as they tried to fit the oversized armor on David. Surely he couldn't go out there without protection, or so the little people thought. But David knew that God was on his side, so he discarded the armor and dashed out into the valley, picking up five smooth stones. Once Goliath was done talking trash, David hurled a stone at him, nailing him squarely in the head. And that was that. Nope, WWE fans, this one wasn't fake. Goliath was dead, the victim of a kid who had barely reached puberty![11]

Ironically, the strapping King Saul had remained on the sidelines while a mere boy killed the feared enemy giant. David had the courage of a king, but even after his heroic act, he didn't immediately assume the throne. Since Saul was still alive, he refused to step over him. Instead, David would live the life of a fugitive for the next fourteen to sixteen years. But it wasn't wasted time. As he hid out in caves, feigned madness, and ducked hurled javelins, David learned the same lesson God attempted to teach Israel: Trust me; obey me.[12]

"I know the odds are against you; you're clearly the underdog," God seemed to say. "I know you looked ridiculous going against Goliath with nothing but five smooth stones in your hand. I know everyone heard the laughter from the Philistine soldiers as they stood ready to destroy Israel. They were just waiting for Goliath to make quick work of you so they could launch the attack. But you saw what happened, so continue to trust me."

I can't help but think that when David finally sat on the throne and breathed a sigh of relief at the thought of not having to keep running from Saul, he reflected on the last fourteen or so years. A dead Goliath. A dead Saul. From a shepherd to a king.

Score another one for the little people.

We see it again and again in the sacred narrative and throughout history. God has always used the unknowns, the least likely, the little people. The prophets—guys like Ezekiel and Jeremiah—were the laughingstock of Israel. Daniel and his three buddies beat the odds and moved up the corporate ladder of Babylon, leaning on God to do big things along the way. Even Jesus. Yeah, I know, he was God in the flesh. But of all the places he could have come from, he chose the tiny village of Nazareth. And his looks? Forget about it. The prophet Isaiah wrote of Jesus, "He had no beauty or majesty to attract us to him, nothing in his appearance that we should desire him."[13] The Jews of the first century rejected Jesus because he didn't look or act like nobility.

And think about the men Jesus selected to follow him and to lay the foundation for the church after he returned to heaven. They were uneducated—a fact they were constantly reminded of by the religious and intellectual elite. These guys couldn't get jobs as youth pastors in most large churches today, because they had no graduate degrees. But their effectiveness and impact is unparalleled! Nearly two thousand years later, we pore over their sermons. We study their lives. We examine their writings!

Score yet another one for the little people.

I recently read the Gospels again, paying careful attention to the ministry of Jesus. One thing that immediately jumped out was the type of people Jesus hung out with. While he was in the home of a Pharisee named Simon, a woman ventured in. She was known as the town whore. In an erotic, culturally inappropriate gesture, she untied her hair, letting it fall to her shoulders. (One scholar has noted that such an action was the social equivalent of someone going topless today.[14]) In another violation of social correctness, the woman anointed the feet of Jesus, ignoring the appalled Pharisees whose bread-filled hands had come to a screeching halt halfway to their mouths. And Jesus? He wasn't even rattled. Instead, he told his host a story to illustrate that the woman was showing great love for Jesus because her many sins had been forgiven, while Simon, who had been forgiven little, showed little love.[15]

A woman who is well-known for loose morals can rightly be considered one of the little people, but what about a man who was, literally, a "little" person? Walking along one day, Jesus saw a short man by the name of Zacchaeus, who had climbed a tree so he could survey Jesus's movements. Zacchaeus was working for the Roman IRS, conning everyone and their mother to get them to pay more taxes than they really owed. Because of the con, and because he pocketed the difference, he was the object of everyone's scorn.

Jesus was passing through town that day, but he didn't ignore this crooked little man. Nope, he invited himself to dinner at the tax collector's house.[16] Dinner with such a man was nothing new to Jesus. He had called another tax collector, Levi (later named Matthew), to be his disciple. Jesus had a habit of sharing meals with tax collectors and other despised people of that day, leading the Pharisees to wonder aloud, "How can he eat with such sinners?"[17]

Back then the people you ate with said a lot about who you were. The idea behind the maxim "birds of a feather flock together" was never more true than in first-century Palestine. Mealtime was not about nourishment; it was a time to make a statement about social status. Who you ate your bread and fish with was a strong statement either about who you were or who you aspired to be.

It's no wonder, then, that Jesus constantly shared meals with the little people. He was making a statement: "You prostitutes and tax collectors really matter to me. I care about you." They may have been social outcasts, but in the presence of the Messiah, they were the most important people on earth.

As I continued to read through the pages of Jesus's life, I noticed the glaring contrast between the little people and the Pharisees, the people who considered themselves to be much bigger than they really were. While Jesus took great delight in lifting up the heads of the little people, he seemed to take equally great delight in knocking the Pharisees down a notch or two. He mended the spirit of a broken and sorrowful prostitute by saying, "Neither do I condemn you; go and sin no more."[18] But he called the arrogant Pharisees "whitewashed tombs…full of dead men's bones."[19] Then there was the impoverished widow who gave an offering at the Temple in Jerusalem. Her meager offering was considered chump change by the Pharisees. But Jesus honored her gift as an example of what *real* giving was.[20] Jesus looked into the eyes of his followers and pleaded with them not to be like the Pharisees, who loved to give money, pray, and fast in public so they would be praised by people rather than God.[21]

Caught in the middle between the little people and the prideful Pharisees, the disciples were constantly reminded by Jesus to be like the little people. When he caught his followers arguing about which of them was the greatest, Jesus told them that the greatest person is the one who is the least, that the key to being big is found paradoxically in being little.[22] To underscore his message, Jesus took a little child in his arms and said, "Unless you change and become like little children, you will never enter the kingdom of heaven."[23]

When his disciples deemed children to be too insignificant for Jesus to waste his time on, Jesus chided his followers, saying, "Let the little children come to me…for the kingdom of heaven belongs to such as these." Then he blessed the children, placing his hands on their heads.[24]

Jesus's words must have come across to the disciples like another one of those confusing parables. But his message was clear: Being little in spirit is a prerequisite for intimate, sacred communion with the Father! The Gospels affirm the message that God has always had a soft spot in his heart for the little people.

YOU AND I ARE LITTLE PEOPLE

Darius and I had both finished our breakfast, and he was about to finish his second cup of coffee. He looked across the table and said, "Listening to the way you explain things—how God sides with those who are weak and the social outcasts and all—makes me wonder why my old pastor never broke it down like that when I was growing up.

"You're right about all of us cheering for the underdog," he continued. "I know I love stories where the little guy comes out on top—the whole rags to riches thing. It really does inspire me. I remember watching *Rocky* and leaving the theater feeling like I could beat up any big, bad guy at school. But as I got older, I guess I got more realistic. Don't take this the wrong way, but a lot of what you say, while it's inspiring, still sounds like a fairy tale. Do you get what I'm saying?"

"I sure do," I said. "It's like, okay, David killed Goliath, and the children of Israel walked through the Red Sea on dry land, but what in the world does that have to do with me?"

"Exactly!"

Why should it matter to us that God smiles on little people? Two reasons come to mind. First, because God uses little people who rely on him to do God-sized things. And second, in God's eyes we *all* number among the little people, but sadly, many of us don't realize this because we have an inaccurate, inflated view of ourselves.

The people God has used to do God-sized things have been those who've never lost touch with their innate insignificance. They've always leaned on God with the dependence of a five-year-old, and they remember the lessons of their past. Moses remembered what he learned during forty years of tending sheep in Midian. David remembered the years of frustration while he was on the run from King Saul. And Israel remembered the forty years of wandering in the wilderness. Such experiences constantly reminded Moses, David, and Israel of how big God is and how little they were. Those experiences were, as my father calls them, "holy handicaps" that kept them dependent on the sacred God.

Paul wrestled with his own holy handicap. He referred to it as a "thorn in [the] flesh."[25] Like a nagging splinter that was embedded too deep to remove, Paul's thorn in the flesh constantly reminded him of how little he was. Over time he learned to thank God for his thorn. With great appreciation he said, "To keep me from becoming conceited because of these surpassingly great revelations, there was given me a thorn in my flesh, a messenger of Satan, to torment me. Three times I pleaded with the Lord to take it away from me. But he said to me, 'My grace is sufficient for you, for my power is made perfect in weakness.'"[26]

There it is. Paul praised God for his thorn (what it was, we don't know) because it constantly reminded him of his need for God. Anytime he was tempted to become conceited when throngs of people came to Christ through one of his stirring sermons, Paul would remember the thorn and give thanks to God. When he was done giving a convincing defense of the gospel to the world's intellectual elite, the thorn was there to help put things back in perspective. The thorn kept Paul humble.

Humility goes a long way with God. In fact, humility is the primary characteristic of the little people whom God decides to use. James, the brother of Jesus, issued this instruction, which is linked to a promise from God: "Humble yourselves before the Lord, and he will lift you up."[27]

It's human nature to dwell on our strengths and cover up our weaknesses. But that's putting things backward. The sacred narrative teaches us to never lose sight of our weaknesses, because it's through the lens of our deficiencies that God's leading in our lives becomes clear. I once heard Bishop Eddie Long say that "our mess becomes the fertilizer God uses to grow us." The little people—the ones God uses—don't rejoice in their "mess," but they never forget it. It's what helps them remember, "I'm little; God's big."

When I moved to California to attend seminary and began working at a church, my father called me from South Africa to give me a word of advice. He said, "Son, when you get out there, remember the little people." I was going to be working at a church that had a lot of famous people in the congregation. My father was concerned that I would become so enamored with the stars that I would forget the little people. While I tried to follow that advice as best I could, I've come to see a different application of it. Could it be that remembering the little people is God's message to us about *ourselves?* Maybe we should put a bumper sticker on our cars that reads, "I'm the little person!" Oh, that God would grant us little irremovable splinters that constantly remind us we are the little people who daily need a big God.

I've always been intrigued by the life of Mother Teresa. While she changed her name from Agnes Gonxha Bojaxhiu to Mother Teresa, one thing that never changed about this remarkable woman was her incredible heart for the poor and hurting—the little people. Her intercession on behalf of social outcasts has become known throughout the world. From leper colonies to hospices, she surrounded herself with the little people.

Her journey as spokeswoman and heroine for the little people of the earth brought her before presidents, kings, princes, and even dictators. From Fidel Castro to Bill Clinton, everyone seemed more than willing to help the little woman from Calcutta.

Bob Geldof, leader of the Irish rock band the Boomtown Rats, tells the story of when he first met Mother Teresa. Geldof was known for using profane language, but he managed to clean that up when his path crossed with Mother Teresa. He was helping raise funds for the little people of Africa through a project called Band Aid. Geldof recalls how astonished he was when he realized how short Mother Teresa was—he towered a couple of feet over her. Yet in spite of her small size, he found himself overwhelmed by her presence. Not knowing quite what to do, the rock star bent down to plant a kiss on the sweet old saint's face. Recalling her reaction, Geldof notes, "She bent her head so swiftly that I was obliged to kiss the top of her wimple. It disturbed me. I found out later that she only lets *lepers* kiss her."[28]

The type of person the world deems as big—such as a rock star about to take the stage at a huge concert—made no special impression on Mother Teresa. She refused his kiss. That privilege was reserved for the little people. And like Mother Teresa, God has always rejected those who thought they were bigger than they were. He's not interested in their kisses.

But who were the ones God turned his cheek toward? Moses. David. Israel. A prostitute. Tax collectors. Lepers. The disciples. A persecutor named Saul. Young children. Like Mother Teresa, God reserves his face for the little people.

chapter five

SOMETHING BIGGER

Why We're Convinced There Has to Be More

Remember who you are.

—CRAWFORD LORITTS JR.

Here is the conclusion of the matter: Fear God and keep his commandments, for this is the whole duty of man.

—KING SOLOMON (Ecclesiastes 12:13)

S o you'd consider yourself a little person, huh?" Darius said with a smirk.

"Yeah, I would," I started to say, until I caught his joke. He was eyeing my stomach when he asked the question. Darius had been after me to go to the gym with him so he could whip me into shape.

"I'll go," I said.

"When?"

"Whenever you've got time."

Smiling, he said, "There's no time like the present."

We got in his car and headed to the gym for what I thought would be a quick workout. It was anything but. Afterward I collapsed on the bench in the locker room, exhausted and sore. And Darius was enjoying every minute of it.

"Tired, old man?"

"Hey, I'm only a few years older than you. And, yes, I'm tired." Rubbing my shoulder I said, "You really put it to me out there."

"Oh, that was light," he said. "Wait until next time."

"Next time?"

"Yeah. I figure I'll share my knowledge and expertise on the body if you'll keep schooling me on the Bible."

"Fair enough," I said. "I just wish my part inflicted as much pain on you as you put on me today."

Darius sat down next to me. "It's pretty interesting to think that I'm a 'little person,' as you would say. Just like Rahab or David was. I've never thought of it that way. You know those Sunday-school days with the big cutout Bible characters they'd put on the flannel board, and all the stories they told? When I was a kid, I thought those people were huge superheroes, doing things I could never even dream about doing. But you showed me their humanity and their weaknesses, and that has made me think I could do some big things, you know?"

"You've just described me as well as you," I said. "Every time I think about the little-people theme in the sacred narrative, I'm reminded of my own family history."

My great-great-grandfather was a slave named Peter Loritts. He worked on plantations in North Carolina. He couldn't read or write, but one thing he had going for him was an incredible love for God, a love that would sustain him through years of being "owned" by other men.

The people who owned my ancestors had more compassion than many slaveholders. They freed my great-great-grandfather long before Abraham Lincoln issued the Emancipation Proclamation. With newfound freedom, Peter migrated to Catawba County, North Carolina, purchased some land, and built the family homestead. There this illiterate man would sit on a rocking chair on his porch and have his children read to him over and over again from the Scriptures. In this way, the old man was able to memorize long portions of the sacred narrative.

Peter had a son named Milton, my great-grandfather. Like his father, Milton had an incredible love and zeal for God, which was evident in his tireless work for the old AME Zion Church in Conover, North Carolina, where he volunteered for years as Sunday-school superintendent.

Milton was a busy man with fourteen kids. Unable to go to marriage conferences or buy any how-to-have-a-better-family books, Milton still excelled as a father and influenced both his family and others for God. In fact, all fourteen of his kids put their faith in Jesus Christ.

Milton's youngest boy, Crawford Wheeler Loritts Sr., was my grand-father. Long before Jackie Robinson broke the color barrier in the major leagues, Hambone, as they called my grandfather, played baseball in the Negro Leagues. I still remember the stories he told as he rocked on his porch in Roanoke, Virginia. I loved hearing him talk about playing ball in the same league as Josh Gibson and Satchel Paige.

To support his family my grandfather worked in the coal mines in the off-season. One day tragedy struck when a dynamite blast knocked out one of his eyes. Just like that, old Hambone's baseball days were over. But he was okay; he had his faith to sustain him. He knew he was play-ing for someone bigger and something greater.

My grandfather's only son is my father, Crawford Wheeler Loritts Jr., one of the most godly men I know. He travels throughout the world, pro-claiming the gospel of Jesus Christ. I can't count the number of people who have told me about the influence my father has had on them.

My father is not perfect, but even in his faults he's amazing. I was sit-ting in class as a kid one day when my father came to the school to apol-ogize for something he'd falsely accused me of. A big reason why I do what I do today is because of my dad's godly influence.

My father used to say something that initially irked me, but the older I got the more sense it made. He would normally issue this reminder just as he was handing me the car keys so I could go on a date or hang with my friends. He'd say, "Son, remember who you are."

At first I just shrugged, happy to have the keys to the Ford Aerostar. (Can you believe I took that thing to the prom?) But as the night wore on, I'd sometimes find myself in compromising situations, and those words would shout in my soul—as if someone were turning up the volume. And more times than not, even when I really wanted to do something bad, I didn't, because of that piercing, perplexing statement.

My father wasn't telling me to remember my locker combination or my address. He was reminding me that my last name is Loritts, and because of that, a lot was expected of me. Now that I'm a father myself, I find that life only gets more complicated. There's the occasional temptation to fudge on an income tax return, have a one-night stand that my wife would probably never know about, tell a lie that might get me out of an awkward situation. Of course, I still mess up and sin just like everyone else. But when I'm tempted to do something, I get a vision of my great-great-grandfather, Peter Loritts, rocking in his chair, listening to his kids read him the Bible. Or I picture Milton Loritts, my great-grandfather, having family devotions with all fourteen of his kids.

My dad's words ring in my ears. I have a heritage. Men have gone before me who loved and served God, and they have passed on to me a spiritual legacy that is worth so much more than pursuing the temporary pleasures of life. My dad wanted me to know that there is someone bigger out there, something much greater at stake than having a good time.

That awareness of someone bigger and something greater is what Solomon, the third king of Israel, alluded to in his personal memoirs: the book of Ecclesiastes. The wise old man—reflecting on his life—said of God, "He has…set eternity in the hearts of men."[1] Like the eerie feeling you sometimes get that someone is watching you, Solomon says we all have an awareness that someone bigger than us is watching. As little people, we are acutely aware of someone bigger—even if we don't believe in God or a "higher power."

Muslims call that someone Allah. George Lucas simply called this power "the Force." But practically all of humanity knows someone bigger is out there. They may not know what to call this being, but they have a distinct inner sense that someone bigger is there. We can't avoid it, since eternity has been etched on our hearts.

A SENSE OF ETERNITY

"Eternity," I said. "That's something worth thinking about."

"You know, that's a big part of why I still want to get together with you," Darius said, barely above a whisper. "Whatever I do, no matter how awful it is, I can identify with that old king…what'd you say his name was?"

"Solomon."

"Yeah, I can identify with what Solomon said. 'God has put eternity in our hearts.' That's big. See, I know God is out there. And my boys do too, and they're pretty rough."

"You know what's funny about what you just said, Darius? Some of the roughest guys in the hip-hop game—guys like Notorious BIG (Biggie) and Tupac Shakur—had a strong awareness of God. But both of these guys could have been poster children for immorality and depravity. Whether it was life imitating art or art imitating life, we know they would never be held up as models of exemplary character and conduct.

"Both were adulterers. Tupac even wrote a song about his supposed adulterous affair with Biggie's wife, Faith Evans. Biggie used to sell drugs, something he likewise wrote songs about. Tupac even declared that he looked forward to the day when he could party with all his homies in hell."

"Yeah, I know all that," Darius said. "So what's the point?"

"The point is that both of these guys had an awareness of eternity.

Biggie's last album was called *Life After Death*. Throughout the album he talks about dying and what happens next. Tupac, even more than Biggie, obsessed about the afterlife. Not only did he anticipate an eternity in hell, but he wrote a song that asks the question, 'I wonder if heaven got a ghetto?'[2] These two notorious rappers had eternity etched across their hearts."

I don't mean to single out rappers. The same thing is true of the rest of us. Questions about the afterlife and musings about someone or something greater than us are common among students, computer programmers, athletes, homemakers, and small-business owners. We all ponder deeply the ultimate meaning of life.

Watch a college football game or an NFL game, and you'll see a running back enter the end zone and raise his index finger in recognition of God. A baseball player clears the fence with a 420-foot blast, pounds his chest, and blows a kiss with his two fingers toward the heavens. A team bows in the locker room to recite the Lord's Prayer before a game. For some, these rituals may be nothing more than good luck charms. But somewhere deep inside is the recognition that someone or something is out there, and that reveals the fingerprint of the One who designed our souls.

I recently spoke to about one hundred college students from Southern California. During breaks from speaking I went outside to enjoy the breathtaking beauty of Bass Lake, to gaze at the distant hills, and to stare in wonder at the stars. On the final evening of the conference, I kept wondering, *How can anyone look at this and not come away believing there's a God?* To be an atheist is to live in denial of God's fingerprint in creation and on our hearts.

And the fact of eternity brings us back to the theme of little people in the sacred narrative. Little people have been propelled to do big things for God because the word *eternity* is scribbled across their hearts. The little people who have done truly significant things for a big God could not turn a deaf ear to the truth their souls were declaring. A growing inner dissatisfaction would not let them rest until they did huge things for a huge God.

In the New Testament, Peter, James, and John were just ordinary fishermen. Every day except the Jewish Sabbath their schedule was the same—unless the weather dictated something different. They sat in a boat and cast their nets into the Sea of Galilee. Sometimes they were successful; many times they weren't.

They'd had one of their worst days ever as they pulled their boats toward shore—the day the teacher showed up. Jesus told these exhausted men to put out their nets one last time. After an initial objection—they told Jesus about their long, unprofitable night—these polite Jewish men obliged the rabbi. Following the instructions of this novice, they were amazed to catch so many fish that the boat began to sink under the load and they needed help from their partners.[3]

Sensing the significance of the moment, Jesus made one more request. "Come, follow me...and I will make you fishers of men."[4] That's it. No PowerPoint presentation. No "think it over and discuss it with your wives, then get back to me." Just "come." And remarkably, the sacred narrative records that these men left everything they had—boats, nets, and other gear—and followed Jesus. There were no questions about salary, retirement plans, or benefits packages. No thought of where they would live. They just left.

Why?

The Spirit of God was working in their hearts to bring about God's will. I'm convinced that when Jesus said, "Follow me," an alarm went off in their souls that said, "That's it! That's what I'm supposed to do." Prior to the rabbi's invitation, they probably thought they'd spend the balance of their days in their boats, eventually passing them on to their children who would do the same with their kids. On and on it would go. And there you have it: Little people doing little things while eternity was screaming in their souls!

Or take Levi. He sat in his tax-collection booth making a nice living. Not an ethical living, necessarily, but a comfortable living. He exacted several percentage points above the required tax rate so he could line his own pockets. He was despised for working for "the man," but that was nothing new. He had a big home and all the luxuries of life. Still, something was missing.

Jesus showed up one day. Scripture doesn't quote any long dialogue between the two. And there's no big explanation on Jesus's part. Just the same two words that retired three fishermen: "Follow me." Levi left everything behind and followed the Savior. Sure, he could have stayed in his tax-collection booth continuing to do little things, but his ears were picking up the ringing of the word *eternity*. He couldn't ignore it.[5]

Much of my time is spent over cups of coffee, talking with people who are wrestling with the deeper issues of life. Their number one question has nothing to do with sex or dating, although those issues are discussed. And it's not finances or marriage. The number one question they're wrestling with has to do with purpose: "Why am I here?"

Most were brought up to believe that college and even grad school were a must. Get the education so you can get the great job that will get you the money you need to buy a nice house and a new SUV. Have kids, take nice vacations, enjoy life. That's living!

So they graduate, get the job, start making the money, and begin to move up the corporate ladder. They get married, buy their first home, and then one morning the alarm clock goes off. They've followed the rules, but what does it all mean? There's an empty feeling in the pit of their stomach. They look around at the family, house, job, and possessions and wonder, *Is this* really *it?* Like Levi sitting in the tax booth, they've come to conclude that there *must* be more to life than this.

That was exactly the message of King Solomon as he recorded his ruminations on life's meaning and purpose. Real life is not found in the things of this world. And that idea is pretty impressive coming from a guy who, by today's standards, was a billionaire many times over!

Ecclesiastes is a sad book. As Solomon critiques his life, what comes bleeding out of the pages is simply, "Don't be like me. Don't try to fill the hole in your soul with the things I sought." He was a man of great excess. Everything Solomon did had to be extravagant. Money? Billions. Women? Try a thousand. Homes? Palatial—it took twice as long to build his palace as it took to build the Temple in Jerusalem.

Like so many today, Solomon woke up one morning and looked at his life. He perused the beautiful grounds of his estate and said, "That's it?" As he sipped tea and surveyed his empire, the hole in his soul widened. The world's wisest man had paradoxically spent his life pursuing foolishness. Although he was huge in the eyes of the world, in God's eyes he was just another little person pursuing little things. He had sought to mute the word *eternity* that was calling out from within him, but in the end he couldn't ignore it.[6]

I love shows like A&E's *Biography* and VH1's *Behind the Music*. These shows reveal the lives of the rich and famous—those who've enjoyed incredible success by human standards. I've looked with amazement at the wealth of Howard Hughes, the musical giftedness of Billie Holiday, and the political power of John F. Kennedy. Yet what has really captivated me has been the paradoxical nature of the lives of the people who are profiled.

They seemingly had it all, but they were some of the most miserable souls on the planet. People marveled at the wealth of Howard Hughes, yet he lived in seclusion in a dark hotel room—completely isolated from life. Music fans couldn't get enough of Billie Holiday's smooth, emotional singing, and yet she spent years going from man to man, desperately longing to be loved.[7] Americans were dazzled by the grace and power of JFK, even dubbing his tenure in office "Camelot," but what they didn't see were all the affairs that threatened to destroy his marriage and America's perception of him and the First Family.

Howard Hughes and Billie Holiday are modern examples of Solomon's message. Stuff doesn't satisfy. And nothing—absolutely nothing—can plug the hole in our soul that only God was meant to fill.

We all know what it's like to cut deals with God, such as "Let me get that car, and then I'll be satisfied." Or "Let me find a good husband, and then I'll be happy." So we buy the car or get married, and then we're back at the bargaining table cutting another deal. "Please God, just get me that promotion at work, and then I'll be set." If there's one truth we've found to be especially true, it's this: Nothing is ever enough. That's human nature.

JESUS AND MEANING

The Messiah issued a simple invitation, one that forced people to make a quick and clear decision: Either acknowledge the voice of eternity and live in its light or keep trying to fill the hole in your soul with the things of this world. This was not a both/and proposition. It was either/or. The disciples made the cut, jumping from the curious crowd to the committed core. They followed Jesus not because of promised blessings or benefits, but because they heard the ring of eternity and knew it was true. They couldn't live the rest of their lives apart from Jesus.

But not everyone chose to follow the pull of eternity. The rich young ruler, whose story is told in Mark 10, was a religious person. He knew the law and tried to keep all the rules and commandments. But there was still a hole in his soul. He had money and a nice home. He was a man of affluence. But his ears were still numb with the ringing of eternity.

"What must I do to inherit eternal life?" was his question as he stood face to face with Jesus. In an effort to expose the hole in the man's soul,

Jesus gave him two propositions. The first was an appeal to the Jewish Law. "Follow the Law and you'll be fine!" The young man shook his head: "Tried it, doesn't work." Finally Jesus told him: "Go home, sell all your possessions, and give to the poor. Then you'll be ready to follow me." Jesus's answer couldn't have been much clearer, could it? But this invitation had a major downside. The young man would have to let go of substantial riches. So he went away sad because he was unwilling to leave his toys behind.[8]

Responding to Jesus's invitation is not both/and; it's either/or.

As the rich young ruler chose possessions over eternity, Jesus wanted his disciples to understand that it's incredibly difficult for a rich person to enter the Kingdom of God. Once a person embraces a life that is centered on possessions, it's hard to part with the toys, to leave everything behind and follow Jesus.

Darius seemed disturbed by what I'd been saying. It looked as if I had touched a nerve.

"Wait a minute," he said. "You mean to tell me that to follow God means I can't have nice things?"

"Now where did you get that?"

"From the story you just told. I mean, by no stretch am I rich, but I definitely plan on gettin' mine!"

"Gettin' your what?"

"You know, a tight Mercedes, a fat house, and, of course, a gorgeous wife. That may take some time, but that's where I'm headed."

"Darius, there's nothing wrong with having those things, as long as they don't become your number one pursuit."

"But you said Jesus told this man that unless he sold all his stuff and gave the money to the poor, he wouldn't be ready to follow God."

"You're partially right."

Darius objected, "But that's what you said!"

"Look at the story in its context. We know that in the end the man said, in so many words, 'I can't do that.' When he refused to sell his possessions, the real point was made. And it has nothing to do with whether it's possible to have nice things and still follow Christ. The real point is that this man loved his money and possessions more than he loved God. And in the end, he chose his stuff over the journey with God."

"So you're saying Jesus has to be number one, ahead of everything else," Darius said. "That's definitely not what I hear from the preachers on TV. I sometimes watch cable on Sunday morning, and some of these guys can show from the Bible that God wants us to have all of this stuff. They make it sound like the really spiritual people are the ones who have the big cars and fine clothes. Man, just look at how these preachers dress! And what's the word they keep saying over and over?"

"Prosperity."

Darius's eyes lighted up. "That's it! Now you're telling me that Jesus said just the opposite from what I'm hearing from these preachers. So somebody's got it wrong."

"Well, I'm not going to go off on all the problems with 'prosperity theology.' But I draw the line when preachers make it seem like the ultimate goal of Christianity is for people to have all the trinkets they want. When you compare that against what the sacred narrative has to say about priorities and commitments in life, that teaching is just wrong. God wants us to treasure him first, ahead of everything else in life. What's sad about the church in America is that too many people want to follow Jesus because they think it will give them a life of ease and convenience. They're looking for something that Jesus never promised, and because of that, they'll die never having experienced true fulfillment. They might get a bigger bank account, but their life won't have meaning."

"Okay," Darius said, "then how do you get fulfillment and meaning?"
"Good question," I said.

The Apostle Paul Considers the End of Life

Unlike Solomon, when the apostle Paul stood on the brink of death, he could look back on his life with a sense of satisfaction. Writing his own eulogy, he told his protégé, Timothy, "For I am already being poured out like a drink offering, and the time has come for my departure. I have fought the good fight, I have finished the race, I have kept the faith."[9] Paul had to have breathed a sigh of relief as he reflected on a life well lived—a life pursuing what really mattered.

He told Timothy that the time had come for his departure. In the language that Paul was writing in, the word for "departure" had to do with a boat that was tied to a dock. When it came time for the boat to set sail, someone would cut the rope, releasing the boat to the sea.

In a similar fashion Paul likened his life to a boat that has been tied to the dock of humanity. As he stared death in the face, Paul knew that very soon his ropes would be cut, and he would be released to set sail on the seas of eternity. And yet he departed with no regrets because he had spent his life pursuing what really mattered—living in light of the Someone who is greater than we are. He hadn't been consumed with piling stuff on the dock, trying to find meaning in money or possessions.

Cars, homes, clothes, retirement plans, promotions, bonuses, a spouse, children. When we die we will leave them all at the dock. None of our stuff is coming with us into the afterlife.

Another apostle, Peter, said that we are merely strangers or aliens passing through this life. This world is not all there is.[10] Jesus taught us to store up treasures in heaven and to seek the Kingdom of God ahead of everything else, because this life is not the end of the story.[11] And King

Solomon ended his memoirs by urging us to fear God and keep his commandments.[12]

The sacred narrative screams at us to acknowledge the ever-widening hole in our soul that has written across it in bold letters just one word: ETERNITY.

DYING WITH REGRETS

Whether or not you know her music, we can all learn from one of the most famous and most beloved singers of the last century. Eleanor Harris was born on April 7, 1915, to Sadie Harris and Clarence Holiday. Not long after she was born, her father abandoned the family to pursue his first love—music. Left without a strong parental influence to guide her, Eleanor fell victim to tragic circumstances. She was raped at age eleven, and during her teens she spent several stints in jail for prostitution. Yet her incredible love for music, especially a fairly new genre called jazz, kept her from losing all hope.

One evening she was filling in for a singer named Monette Moore at a Harlem club. A record producer named John Hammond was there to hear Moore but found himself completely taken with the smooth, emotional voice of Eleanor Harris. At the end of her set, he offered her a recording contract. Eleanor signed, and soon after, Hammond decided to change her name to Billie Holiday.

Holiday circled the globe, singing to sold-out venues. She was accompanied by the likes of Count Basie, Louis Armstrong, and Duke Ellington. She recorded such songs as the socially daring "Strange Fruit," along with "God Bless the Child" and many others. Billie could sing the blues!

And she didn't just *sing* the blues, she *lived* the blues. She was an immoral woman who went from man to man, and she even dabbled in lesbianism. She was addicted to drugs and alcohol.

She died on July 17, 1959, at only forty-four years of age. And she died in shame—chained to her bed, under house arrest for possession of drugs.[13]

What was going through Billie Holiday's mind those last, fleeting moments of her life? She must have been thinking, *If only I had avoided this* or *If I could do it all over, I'd change a lot of things.*

Billie Holiday died with a lot of regrets because she chose to ignore what her soul longed for most. She pressed "mute" on the echoes of eternity in her soul.

chapter six

GLORIA DEO

Bringing a Smile to God's Face

When I run, I feel his pleasure.

—OLYMPIC ATHLETE ERIC LIDDELL, *Chariots of Fire*

So whether you eat or drink or whatever you do, do it all for the glory of God.

—PAUL THE APOSTLE (1 Corinthians 10:31)

Darius had gotten quiet as our conversation ended that day in the locker room. The notion of pursuing God first, even if it meant giving up "the good life," bothered him. To relieve the awkwardness, we talked about sports for a while before leaving the gym for home.

Several weeks since our last conversation, I hadn't heard from Darius. I'd tried calling him and left messages, but I never heard back. I wondered if I'd really offended him. It's not uncommon for God's story to make us feel uncomfortable. But it seemed as though Darius and I had more in common than just an occasional appointment to talk and have coffee. It felt as if we shared some of the same dreams and goals in life: to make life count; not to just exist.

That week I was speaking to the church's Sunday-night young-adult group, and as I walked to the lectern, I noticed Darius sitting in the back.

I was glad he was there, but then I realized that my sermon was about glorifying God, not an easy subject for any of us to deal with. I don't remember everything I said that night, but here's the basic outline.

MAKING GOD SMILE

One of my favorite movies is *Chariots of Fire,* released in the early eighties. It tells the story of two very different men who ran in the 1924 Olympics. One was Harold Abrahams, a Jew who was running for much more than a medal. He was running to prove to the world that Jews are not inferior.

The other athlete was Eric Liddell. Like Abrahams, he was running for far more than a medal. Liddell was a Christian who lived in the tension between his faith and the demands of the world. At times this tension seemed to cross inappropriate boundaries, or so his sister thought.

Liddell was planning to serve on the mission field, just like his parents did. His sister was frustrated because she felt that his running was preventing him from diving headfirst into mission work.

At one point, she asks him, "Eric, why do you run?"

His reply was simple: "When I run, I feel his [God's] pleasure."[1]

I was eight years old when I first saw this film, and I failed to understand the gravity of those words. But over the years, as I've pulled out the old videocassette and watched it again, I find myself anxiously anticipating those words: "When I run, I feel his pleasure."

As Liddell ran, it was as if he could see God smile. Running brought him ultimate fulfillment and satisfaction because he was doing what his Maker had destined him to do.

What will determine whether you will die having lived a wasted life or the abundant life God desires for you is this: choosing to live in such a way that God gets maximum glory from your life. The glory of God is the only turf that can fill the divot in your soul. Listen to these passages from the sacred narrative:

Ascribe to the LORD glory and strength. Ascribe to the LORD the
glory due his name.[2]

For from him and through him and to him are all things. To him
be the glory forever![3]

So whether you eat or drink or whatever you do, do it all for the
glory of God.[4]

It's clear that we are created for God's glory and pleasure. Our purpose is to bring a smile to God's face!

The concept of glory in biblical times was that of weight. In the
ancient world, things were placed on scales, and the heavier something
was, the more value it had. When it comes to the glory of God, we can't
add any value to who he is. Nothing we do will diminish or increase his
magnificence and splendor. It's like a telescope. Telescopes do not add to
the magnitude of the constellations or the moon; they merely magnify
them by bringing their splendor clearly into view. So when it comes to
glory, we're not adding anything to God. He's already full of wonder and
splendor. We're merely illuminating what is already there.

FACING THE TENSION OF GLORY

For the longest time I struggled with God's demanding that humanity
must give him glory. I pictured him leaning against a wall with a smug
look on his face, shouting, "Go ahead. Tell me how great I am!" Doesn't
that sound arrogant to you?

In the Bible we read God's words, such as "I give grace to the humble"
or "I oppose the proud."[5] He goes as far as saying that arrogance and
pride are "detestable" to him.[6] In fact, arrogance is what got Satan kicked
out of heaven. Pride is what evicted Adam and Eve from Eden.[7] Yet with

God wanting us to always glorify him, he comes across like a self-seeking glory hound.

Who would want to be in a relationship with someone whose primary purpose for existing was getting you to constantly tell him how great he is? Would you put up with this from a friend? Or what if your girlfriend constantly said, "Tell me again how pretty I am!" or "Serve me, serve me!"? After a week or two of that sort of thing, the relationship would fall apart.

Yet we're constantly reminded in the Bible to praise God, to tell him how awesome and beautiful he is. It's enough to make you wonder if God has self-esteem issues.

THE FRAMEWORK FOR GOD'S GLORY

If my wife were to constantly bombard me with questions, baiting me to compliment her on all sorts of things, that would tell me she doesn't *feel loved* by me. Because if I truly loved her, I'd treat her in a way that brings her satisfaction, even if it came at my own expense.[8] That's what love does, and it explains why glory must be seen against the backdrop of love.

It's true that we are created to bring God glory. But that's not the end of the story. We can't talk about God's glory without talking about his great love for us. His love motivates me to praise him. It causes tears to run down my face as I extend my hands in worship before him. Bottom line: I give God glory because he loves me. It's that simple.

The love-motivates-glory principle is seen throughout the sacred narrative and is illustrated beautifully in the life of David. In Psalm 19 he makes it clear that even creation gives glory to God. In another psalm he concludes by saying, "Be exalted, O LORD, in your strength; we will sing and praise your might."[9] In another place, amid great distress, he says, "I will declare your name to my brothers; in the congregation I will praise you."[10] David not only directed others to give glory to God, but his own life was a beautiful exposition of a man who gave glory to God even when he encountered great trouble.

But why?

David loved God deeply, so he couldn't avoid glorifying him. And his incredible love for God was driven by God's indescribable love and goodness toward him. The Father's (Abba's) love becomes the stimulus for our ascribing glory to God, thus fulfilling our purpose. But glory is never the beginning; it is only the by-product of the love relationship that we have with God.

REALIZING OUR NEEDINESS

I worshiped at a large church in Soweto, South Africa, when the evil force of apartheid had just been defeated. In a hot, humid gym, I watched for hours as people gave praise to God and danced before him. There was no air conditioning and not even a piano or organ. Just a few scattered tambourines and about fifteen hundred voices. And that was plenty.

As I surveyed the crowd, my mind went back decades to my grandmother's church in Roanoke, Virginia. There the people would dance and shout, and a few would even take off running as the preacher urged them to remember God's goodness and to give him praise. Visions linger in my mind of my dear Nana rocking back and forth as she whispered over and over, "Thank you, Jesus."

Having worshiped in Soweto and in Roanoke, I pondered the connection between the two churches. The people in both congregations were acutely aware of God's goodness. My Soweto brothers and sisters remembered how God had delivered them—no more tanks rolling through the dusty streets; no more being raided in their squatter camps; no more being denied educational opportunities. God had delivered them, so how could they not give him glory?

My grandmother grew up in Lincolnton, North Carolina, without a father. She endured the ridicule of other children because she was a mixed-race youngster whose father wanted nothing to do with her or her mother. Yet against all odds God had delivered her from a life of shame and disgrace. How could she not give him glory?

People who have suffered are in tune with their need for God and his goodness. In Soweto, I was moved as I heard a woman give public praise to God for the miraculous bus pass he had provided for her earlier that week. I was in shock as I learned of people who walked some twenty miles just to go to church. To these people, giving God glory is almost an obligation because he has been so good to them.

And what about their brothers and sisters here in America?

We focus on the fringe issues. We argue over which songs to sing and whether the organ should be played at the early service. We fight over styles of worship and different expressions of worship and praise. We struggle to lift up our hands before God, mumbling under our breath, "It doesn't take all that. God knows my heart, and that's what really matters." We've become ungrateful and have lost sight of God's goodness and provision for our needs. Worship has become a matter of convenience, not a privilege and an opportunity to give God glory because of his abundant love.

In the first century there was a leper who heard about Jesus. He had heard that Jesus was "in revival" on a hillside with thousands listening to his words, so the leper, in his tattered rags, left the lepers' colony. As he approached the area where Jesus was preaching, he had to shout out, "Unclean, unclean." Mothers clutched their children close, and with every step the leper made toward the crowd, the Pharisees became more infuriated. Who was this "untouchable" to think he could approach them?

But the leper was on a mission, and nothing was going to stop him.

He finally approached Jesus the Messiah. The crowd grew silent as people watched to see what the Teacher would do. *Surely, he's not going to touch this man,* they thought. No one in his right mind touched lepers. The silence turned a bit awkward as the God-man stared into the eyes of this decaying, breathing corpse. But finally the silence was broken when the leper cried out, "Lord, if you are willing, you can make me clean."[11]

Jesus could have healed the man with a word, as he had done before with others. Just declare the man healed and get on with his sermon. But Jesus had a point to make in front of these thousands who pulled back in horror from the leprous man. To protect themselves from disease, society ostracized lepers, putting them in their own colony well outside town. So the people in the crowd assumed that Jesus most certainly was not going to touch this man.

But Jesus extended his hand and touched the untouchable. With a smile on his face as he rested his hand on the leper's shoulder, Jesus said, "I am willing.... Be clean!"[12] Immediately the leper was cured. Once-sagging skin had been restored. There was no more decay, no more odor.

And for the first time in a long time, the man could feel. He felt the tears gently trickle down his cheeks. He felt the warmth of the sun on his skin. He felt the love of God.

As the former leper was about to leave, Jesus said, "Oh, one more thing. Don't tell anyone about this." The leper paused, looked at Jesus, and then took off running. The gospel writer Mark, describing this event, gives us some added information: "Instead he went out and began to talk freely, spreading the news. As a result, Jesus could no longer enter a town openly but stayed outside in lonely places."[13]

The man told so many people what Jesus had done for him that it had a radical impact on Jesus's ministry. Jesus could no longer enter a town openly!

The leper had come face to face with God's love. And the love of Christ became the stimulus for giving God glory.

All of us have received God's love. The fact that I am awake and breathing is a testament to God's love. The ability to enjoy God's creation, to relate with others, all of this points to God's love and the measure of his grace that is given to all people. As creatures who bear the stamp of God's image, how can we do anything else but give back to God what is properly his. He deserves glory.

THE PROBLEM OF PRIDE

There is, of course, a problem. Pride takes the glory God deserves and redirects it to ourselves. Pride is the ultimate violation of our relationship with God. In fact, the very core of sin is pride.

Most of our sins result from conscious choices we make to violate God's nature and his law. Sin doesn't happen by accident; we're always accomplices. Someone mistreats us, so we decide to repay evil for evil. In a heated moment of sexual passion, we decide to ignore the Spirit's voice of guidance, and we commit immorality. We hear a piece of juicy information on someone else, and we decide to spread it around. Basically, we decide to satisfy our desires instead of God's. The common denominator in all sin is pride: We choose ourselves over God.

Pride is the refusal to acknowledge our need for God—that all we have, all we are, and all we could ever hope to be is in God's hands. Too many people fail to recognize their need for God. Whenever people think they are an end unto themselves, they're in a position of pride and arrogance, failing to give God what is rightfully his.

After the September 11, 2001, terrorist attacks in New York and Washington, D.C., people returned to church in massive numbers. They'd been reminded of something. On Monday of that week, people were routinely going about their business, and suddenly the next day, thousands of innocent lives were taken. People were confronted with the fragile nature of life. They were put deeply in touch with their need of God.

Like a light that blinked on and then quickly flickered out, people momentarily recognized their neediness and sought out a place where they might find God. The sound of eternity grew louder in their hearts, and for a while they listened. Then things gradually returned to normal, and people reverted to business as usual. Once again, they decided to take charge of their lives and seek to bestow glory on themselves rather than on God.

But people are always faced with a new crisis, usually on a very personal level. We experience a cancer scare or a family crisis or the loss of someone we love. We find ourselves in need, and we turn to God. Then the crisis fades, and we put ourselves back in the center of our own little world, a world in which God is a far-distant second.

This is not a modern development. We read about the same thing happening in the sacred narrative. In the book of Judges, we get a panoramic view of Israel's on-again, off-again relationship with God. Whenever the Israelites decided to do things their way, they would eventually find themselves in a world of hurt. God would use the crisis to show the people how much they needed him. Then they would cry out to God, giving him glory. God would ease their pain, but soon, convenient amnesia would set in; they would forget their neediness and go back to the same old pattern, a pattern that had a common theme woven into it: pride.

The message God tried to imprint on their hearts was simple: "Remember me always. Whatever you do, don't forget me. Because when you live your lives remembering who I am, you'll give me glory! And that's when you'll see me work in your lives."

All of us can identify with Israel. We know what it's like to turn to God when times are tough and ignore him when things are going well. It's during the good times when we act in pride and bestow on ourselves the one thing that belongs only to God: glory.

Maybe that's why I enjoy *Rocky III* so much. Rocky's old nemesis, Apollo Creed, is helping him train to fight Clubber Lang. But Rocky's heart isn't in it. The way he's training, he's going to get killed in the ring. Apollo tells Rock that he's lost the "eye of the tiger." He's forgotten the days when he was a hungry bum, begging for a shot at the title.

Apollo takes Rocky away from the comforts of home and transports him to the gritty world of inner-city Los Angeles. Rocky needs to be around hungry people, people who haven't already made it. People who have the eye of the tiger. Rocky trains amid needy people and regains his passion and sense of purpose. But before he reached that point, he had to be reminded where he'd come from. He needed to look once again at what life had been like before the glory of becoming heavyweight champion.[14]

It's only when we remember who we are in contrast to who God is—when we are confronted again with our desperate need for God—that we find ourselves in position to do what we were created to do. That's when we find a way to give glory to God.

ORDINARY FOLKS GIVING GOD GLORY

Darius and I left church as soon as I finished speaking, and fortunately we got to the cigar shop before it closed. I had suggested we do something together, and he agreed to go along with my recommendation. The attendant took our jackets, and we found seats toward the back. Darius seemed a bit confused.

"How do you, a man of the cloth, know about this place?" he asked.

"What's up with this man-of-the-cloth thing?"

"Well, maybe my conservative roots are starting to show, but I don't put pastors and stogies in the same category."

"Well, to ease your mind, this isn't a habit or some addiction for me. It's just that I do, on occasion, enjoy a fine cigar."

Just then the attendant came by and asked, "Sir, will you be having your usual?"

Darius looked at me as if to say, "Sure this isn't a habit?"

"I'll go with my usual, and my friend will have an Arturo Fuente—very mild."

The attendant looked at Darius, who simply shrugged his shoulders and said, "Sure."

Soon the cigars came, and we began to talk.

"I've missed you, Darius. Did you get my messages?"

"Yeah." There was an awkward pause. "Okay, I'm not going to make excuses, like I've been real busy. I just haven't called you back because, well, I left our last conversation feeling a little judged."

"You mean after we talked about pursuing God first, ahead of money and possessions?"

"Exactly."

"When you say you felt 'judged,' are you saying you felt like I came down on you?"

"Yeah, although I know you weren't necessarily attacking me personally."

Darius stopped to light his cigar. Then he continued.

"See, my dad was very controlling... Still is. Everything's got to be *his* way. To this day we have problems, even though I moved out years ago. When he offers free advice about something I'm doing or not doing, it just rubs me the wrong way."

"What do you do when he says this stuff?" I asked.

"I get off the phone real quick and don't talk to him for a month or so."

"Sort of like what you did to me."

We laughed.

"Yeah, you're right," Darius said. "So it wasn't really you; it's just that whenever I feel like someone is trying to get me to turn left when I want to go right, it causes all of those issues I got with my old man to come up."

"So what brought you to church tonight?"

"I guess I came around because I started missing our talks and your friendship."

I was relieved to hear that. I worried that I had turned him off to God for good.

"It's like you've flattened everything I ever thought about the Bible," he continued. "I was raised with strict religious rules, and here you and I are leaving church to go smoke some expensive cigars. If my mother found out about this, she'd kill me—and I'm a grown man!"

I set my own cigar down and looked Darius in the eyes.

"I didn't bring you here to try and win cool points with you. I brought you here because it's a quiet place where no one will bug us, and because I enjoy your company. I just like to come here with friends."

We smoked in silence for a while, then Darius raised the topic of my sermon earlier that evening.

"Tell me more about this glory stuff," he said. "You're right, it does seem like God is some kind of egomaniac, consumed with getting perpetual pats on the back. But when you talked about looking at glory in the context of love, that started to make sense."

"But there's a problem, right?" I was waiting for Darius to issue a challenge.

"Yeah, I guess I'm struggling to see what that looks like in somebody's life—other than going to church all the time and singing hymns and stuff. For the person who is a teacher, does that mean he goes into the classroom lifting up his hands in praise to God? Or for the administrative assistant. What does that look like for her? Do you follow me?"

"Sure. I should have explained a little more what glorifying God looks like for ordinary folks like you and me. We give glory to God when we do little things like show up to work on time and do a really bang-up job. I'll give you a personal example. I went to Bible college and got tired of being around Christians all day. So I got a job at the mall, doing retail. On the first day I realized I had my work cut out for me. My boss was gay, the assistant manager was living with her boyfriend, and a couple of my co-workers were into the party scene big time. I decided I wouldn't announce my Christianity until after I'd won several employee contests for sales performance. I wanted them to know I was there to do everything I could to make the store a success.

"I worked my butt off and started winning awards. Soon I was getting questions from my co-workers like, 'Man, you seem to be really into this job, and you do a really great job. Why are you working so hard?' Questions like that were nothing more than doors being flung open for me to talk about my relationship with God. But here's what I want you to see, Darius. Giving God glory is not so much seen in the explicit acts that we do—talking about him, slapping a fish symbol on our car, or raising our hands to him in the end zone after making a touchdown—as much as it is about representing him through consistent character that's in line with his character and nature.

"When I was selling clothes at the mall, I learned that I was the only Bible these people were going to read. I had to ask myself if they were getting an adequate picture of God. Tony Evans, a pastor in Dallas, says if you're a photographer, people should get a clear idea of what God looks like when you capture drama and beauty with your camera. Or if you're a lawyer, people should get a picture of what God looks like when you give everything you've got trying a case."

Darius pointed a finger at me and said, "That's it! That explains why so many people who aren't followers of Christ have a problem with Christians. What Christians say doesn't match how they live. And glorifying God is just as much about what people do as what they say!"

"You're onto something," I said. "Sin in a person's life, including a disconnect between what he says and how he lives, is the biggest deterrent to giving God glory. No matter how you look at it, sin's a problem."

chapter seven

NO LAUGHING MATTER

Sin and the Heart of God

Its victims often ate lunch with their friends and dinner with their ancestors in paradise.

—BOCCACCIO, speaking of the plague

You are proud! Shouldn't you rather have been filled with grief?

—PAUL THE APOSTLE (1 Corinthians 5:2)

D arius was lighting his second cigar when I decided to wade into the difficult but unavoidable subject of sin. I mentioned the topic and asked Darius to hold his questions and objections until I had described what I felt was a dead-on comparison from history. Sin is a spiritual plague that brings death, much like the plagues of the Middle Ages that spread unchecked and decimated the human population.

Darius leaned back in his chair as I reached back into history. In the early 1330s, China stood at the center of world trade. Merchants flocked to her shores to glean from an amazing variety of goods. And when those merchants returned home to countries throughout the known world, they imported the one thing that no one wanted: the bubonic plague.

The plague caused a high fever and painful swelling of the lymph glands, called buboes, thus the name *bubonic*. And because so many

Europeans ventured to China, the continent was devastated by the plague's widespread effects.

The plague worked its way north from Italy all the way to England. It spread with such speed that Boccaccio, the Italian writer, noted that "its victims often ate lunch with their friends and dinner with their ancestors in paradise." During the winters, people breathed a sigh of relief, thinking the disease had vanished. They didn't realize that fleas, which were dormant in the winter, were the primary carriers. With the warmth of spring, the fleas returned—along with the plague.

For years the epidemic spread, with some twenty-five million people succumbing to it—a third of Europe's population. Yet its effects reached far beyond the lives it claimed. The plague brought fear, separating families and neighbors and dividing co-workers.

Then a few centuries later came the influenza epidemic of 1918. The most deadly pandemic our world has ever known, it killed as many as forty million people. Cases of influenza became so dreadfully common that children would skip rope to the rhyme:

I had a little bird,
Its name was Enza.
I opened the window,
And in-flu-enza.[1]

As the flu pandemic wore on, the sight of massive piles of corpses became common. Because there was a shortage of coffins, morticians, and gravediggers, bodies could not receive a proper burial. Commenting on the pandemic, researcher Molly Billings notes, "The public health departments distributed gauze masks to be worn in public. Stores could not hold sales, funerals were limited to 15 minutes. Some towns required a signed certificate to enter.... Those who ignored the flu ordinances had to pay steep fines enforced by extra officers."[2]

As I read Billings's references to people having to wear masks in public, I immediately thought of the SARS (severe acute respiratory syndrome) scare, which made the news in 2003. While it didn't reach epidemic levels, it still claimed enough lives to strike fear in people. The front page of the *New York Times* ran a photograph of a Chinese couple on their wedding day wearing masks to protect themselves from the disease.[3]

Once again fear gripped the world. Missions groups canceled summer trips to Asia because of the threat of SARS. Pets of SARS victims were euthanized in China. Several passenger jets were stopped on runways and held up for hours because of the fear of SARS being spread by infected travelers. Infectious disease on a large scale gets people's attention and changes their outlook and behavior.

The Spiritual Pandemic

There's an epidemic out there, actually a pandemic, whose effects are more widespread than the influenza pandemic of the early twentieth century. It has been around practically since the dawn of time. And it has killed *every* human being born into the world. It's the spiritual pandemic of sin. If you look at things through the lens of the sacred narrative, you'd have to conclude that sin is a pandemic of the worst proportions.

The apostle Paul wrote, "Therefore, just as sin entered the world through one man, and death through sin, and in this way death came to all men, because all sinned."[4] Paul was referring to Adam as the one who introduced sin to the world. Then Paul made a crucial point: Adam's sin was not done in isolation, affecting just him and his wife. Adam's sin had devastating, worldwide implications. Through Adam, all of humanity has been infected with the crippling, terminal disease of sin.

In the ancient Greek language, the language Paul was using, the concept of death was complex. The word for death is the Greek word *thanatos,* and it carries with it the idea of separation.

One kind of death is, obviously, physical. When we die, our spirits separate from our bodies. When followers of Christ die, their bodies stay in the grave, but their spirits go into the presence of God.

There's another aspect to thanatos, though, and that's an eternal separation from God. This applies to people who die without first entering into a personal relationship with God through his Son, Jesus Christ. They'll experience eternity without God in hell. The fire will be painful and the darkness maddening, but for people who spend eternity in hell, the worst part may be that there will be no signs of God there.

Another aspect of thanatos is more temporal in nature. It refers to the momentary separation from God that we all experience because of our sins. Even after we enter into relationship with God, we continue to experience temporary breaches in our journey with him because of our sins. This is a form of death, obviously not final, but it's separation nonetheless.

The plague of sin has more far-reaching effects than the influenza pandemic of 1918. The sin pandemic guarantees the death of every person on earth. No one can escape it.

The pandemic of sin has infected all of humanity not only physically and spiritually but also emotionally and in every other way imaginable. We all have our share of dysfunction in life thanks to the pervasive damage of sin. Divorce, abuse, adultery, greed, lust, gossip—you name it— they all stem from the fact that we're sinners, and sin is the one thing none of us can escape.

People don't die merely of cancer or heart attacks or auto accidents. The common denominator in every death and dysfunction is sin.

WHERE IS OUR FEAR?

With such a devastating pandemic loose in the world, you'd think we'd be scared out of our wits. But it's quite the opposite. We see the sin pandemic but ignore its effects, choosing instead to indulge in it and just take our chances.

Flip on the television. MTV has a show called *Real World*. They take a group of diverse people, mix in a few sex maniacs, stir in someone living an alternative lifestyle, and—*boom!*—they have the "real" world. On any given episode you're likely to see people engaged in some type of sexual immorality or entangled in some other sinful web. The participants seem to enjoy it. The show is popular, in part, because it allows us to laugh at our dysfunction.

Or take another MTV regular, *The Osbournes*. This show is a sad caricature of the modern family. If you watch this show, you hear only about half of the dialogue due to the barrage of f-bombs being dropped from kids and parents alike. The family patriarch is, of course, Ozzy Osbourne, who likes to refer to himself as the Prince of Darkness. The message of this show—like so many others—is that sin is a laughing matter, not a deadly pandemic.

In its blindness to the sin pandemic, the music played on the radio even robs relationships of romance. Think about the Bloodhound Gang song "The Bad Touch." Speaking of sex, they sing, "Let's do it like they do on the Discovery Channel. Gettin' horny now."[5] I can picture the hearts of millions of women melting over this tender metaphor. Talk about romancing the ladies…

The sin pandemic doesn't bring beauty; it brings death. And sadly, it has become a laughing matter in our world.

What About Christians?

Sin affects Christians just as it does everyone else. But since Christians know God, they should have clearer vision when it comes to identifying and avoiding the devastation of the sin pandemic. Sadly, that's not always the case. Seldom do you hear the word *sin* mentioned in church. It's more common for preachers to refer to people's *issues*. Greed is now called prosperity, and hatred is merely emotional dysfunction.

Or listen to the way some Christians talk about how they found Jesus. "I used to smoke weed all day," or "I slept with more than fifty different women." While these statements may be true, it's the attitude behind the remarks that is troubling. Listening to these stories, you don't get the sense that people feel shame about their sin. Instead, they seem to have a sort of romantic fascination with their corrupt past. Like an out-of-shape, middle-aged man talking about his glory days on the gridiron, many Christians have a glimmer in their eyes when they talk about sin instead of feeling regret.

Such a cavalier attitude toward sin doesn't reflect the heart of God as revealed in the sacred narrative. In fact, the chasm between God's attitude toward sin and ours is infinitely wide. Consider these thoughts from the narrative:

> There are six things the LORD hates, seven that are detestable
> to him: haughty eyes, a lying tongue, hands that shed innocent
> blood, a heart that devises wicked schemes, feet that are quick to
> rush into evil, a false witness who pours out lies and a man who
> stirs up dissension among brothers.[6]

> To fear the LORD is to hate evil; I hate pride and arrogance, evil
> behavior and perverse speech.[7]

> Again and again I sent my servants the prophets, who said, "Do
> not do this detestable thing that I hate!" But they did not listen
> or pay attention; they did not turn from their wickedness or stop
> burning incense to other gods. Therefore, my fierce anger was
> poured out; it raged against the towns of Judah and the streets
> of Jerusalem and made them the desolate ruins they are today.[8]

Darius had kept quiet during my anti-sin rant, but now he couldn't sit still.

"So are you saying I should walk around with my head down, afraid to look people in the eye because of my past mistakes?" he asked. "None of us is perfect. You said so yourself. So now why do we have to hang our heads about messing up?"

"There's a difference between letting our past drag us down and taking our sin seriously," I explained. "God takes sin seriously, so we should do the same.

"Think about the consequences that God dealt out in the Old Testament when people sinned," I continued. "The punishment for certain violations of his law was execution. I realize that some of these examples are extreme, but they make a good point when we're thinking about how much God hates sin. The sacred narrative is clear—God doesn't play games when it comes to sin."[9]

"But God knows we're weak and limited and prone to mess up," Darius said. "So why is he so harsh with us when it comes to sin?"

"Well, that gets to the essence of sin," I said. "It's not just an honest mistake or a lapse of judgment. One biblical scholar defines sin as 'any failure to conform to the moral law of God in act, attitude or nature.'[10] The essence of sin is not that we make mistakes. It's a failure on our part to act in humility by conforming our lives to God's will. We put ourselves and our own desires ahead of what God wants for us."

"I remember talking about this before," Darius said. "It's the pride thing again. Are you saying that everything we want to do is wrong, just because we're full of pride? If I were a Christian, would I have to shut down all my desires and remove all the fun from my life? To be honest, that's not a good sales pitch for the Bible."

"It's not a matter of shutting down all the fun," I said. "Instead, it's a process of putting God's desires ahead of our own. God made us so that we could give him glory by living in an intimate love relationship with him. We give God glory when we live in submission to his plans and purposes for us. Every time I share my faith with someone, I'm giving him glory. When I put someone else's well-being ahead of my own, I'm giving him glory. Fulfilling our purpose in life involves obeying God—and that's what gives our lives meaning and brings ultimate satisfaction."

THE CHOICE TO SIN

For the most part sin is a choice we make. We can plead ignorance of the Law, but nine times out of ten, we're lying. Far too many times we choose to go against what we know is right. But why does God get so worked up over our disobeying him?

Think about a person who sleeps with someone he or she isn't married to. It's clear that God prohibits sex outside of marriage, but I don't believe it's adultery alone that's offensive to him. What really ticks him off is the fact that a person chooses to do it when he or she knows God forbids it. The same could be said of lying, stealing, gossiping, and any other sin. Sin is a symptom of a bigger problem: the decision to choose our will over God's.

Because sin is the choice to rebel against God, it makes sense that God responds with hatred toward our sin. To God, sin is not casual and impersonal; it's offensive and highly personal. It violates his character and nature.

I experience some of this with my own children. After my older son, Quentin, turned two, there were times when he would look me right in the eye and say "No!" when I had asked him to do something. Then there were times when I warned him about playing with electrical outlets, and he'd wait until I was out of sight so he could do it anyway.

He still has his moments. And what really gets me upset is not that he touches something he's not supposed to touch or plays with things he's not supposed to play with. What irks me is his doing those things even though I told him not to. My anger is sparked because my will has been violated by the conflicting will of a depraved child.

When any of us chooses to sin, we're elevating our will over God's will for us. When I'm asked a question that puts me in an unflattering light, I can choose to lie. I might avoid temporary embarrassment, but in doing so I'm choosing my own desires over God's desire for me. And God's will has been violated.

Choosing Against the Plague

If we're going to live according to God's will, we must begin by adopting God's attitude toward sin. We must come to hate sin if we hope to make any progress against the sin pandemic.

I was once with another pastor when he was approached by a desperate mother. With tear-filled eyes she begged him to do something about her wayward child. After the pastor asked her a few probing questions, she revealed that her child was addicted to drugs. Looking the distraught woman squarely in the eyes, this pastor asked, "Has he hit rock bottom yet?" In a roundabout way the woman said he hadn't. Very sympathetically the pastor told her that he couldn't do anything for the young man and that she should notify him when her son had hit the bottom.

I initially felt that his response was cold and somewhat terse. *He could have at least met with the man and offered a prayer,* I thought. But the more I pondered his words, the more sense they made. It's a fundamental rule of life: People will not change—especially when it comes to addictions—until they come to a point where they hate their behavior. It must begin with a drastic attitude change.

This was exactly the predicament of the prodigal son in the Bible. He had lived for quite some time in a foreign country. He had wasted his inheritance on a partying lifestyle. Alcohol had become his close friend. Immorality abounded. His days were spent recovering from the previous evening's debauchery, trying to sober up in time for the next evening's festivities.

The cycle of sinfulness ran on until his inheritance ran out. With the depletion of funds came the depletion of friends. And the next thing he knew, the only option he had was to take a job feeding swine. That's when he hit rock bottom. The sacred narrative notes that one day while he was in the pig pen, he "came to his senses." He was now ready to come home to his father, but *only* after he had hit rock bottom.[11]

That's how it is with the sin pandemic. Until we enter into a covenant relationship with God—loving him with all of who we are—we will never adopt his feeling of personal revulsion at our own depravity. We don't have to beat ourselves up over every sin, but we do have to stop taking our sin so lightly. And it helps if we can get a good picture of what our sin does to God.

In 1962, when my father was twelve years old, he was hanging with some troublemakers on the streets of Newark, New Jersey. They were walking home from school, and one of the boys spotted some valuable jewelry that a vendor had mistakenly left out in the open. Unable to pass up this grand opportunity, the boys grabbed some jewelry and took off.

They made their way home as if nothing was wrong. When my dad got to his house, he hid his stolen goods underneath some clothes in a dresser drawer. Several hours later his father came home early from work—something that rarely happened. And not long after, there was a knock on the front door. The police were standing there with the other young boys who had stolen the jewelry.

They informed my dad's father that some jewelry had been stolen, and they had reason to believe his son was involved. With piercing eyes my grandfather asked my dad if it was true, and with a quick, calm lie my father said it wasn't. My dad's next words were not the brightest, but what happened would change his life. My dad called the officers' bluff and told them that if they wanted to check his room, they could. That was an invitation the police couldn't pass up. It wasn't often they were invited in without a search warrant. So off they went, and sure enough the jewelry was found.

Immediately the officers gave my dad's father a choice. Either they could take my dad and the other young thieves in, or my grandfather could deal with the boys himself. Getting his anger under control, my grandfather thanked the police and said he would take the other junior thieves home to their parents.

One by one the boys were dropped off at their homes, with my grandfather describing to the parents what the boys had done. My dad sat silently in the backseat of his father's car, watching each boy being taken to the door of his home. Then when my dad and his father finally got back home, my grandfather told his only boy—almost in a faint whisper—to go downstairs, where spankings were administered. My dad knew he was about to receive the whipping of his life. When his dad finally came downstairs, instead of seeing an angry father, my dad saw a broken man. With tears streaming down his face, my grandfather said, "Boy, I'll die before I ever see you go to jail. You broke my heart."

I must have heard this story twenty or more times as I was growing up. And what always gets me is that the thing my father remembered most was not the spanking he received, but his father's tears. For the first time in his life, he saw his father cry, and my dad never stole another thing.

Sin arouses God's wrath, but it also breaks his heart. Stories from the sacred narrative show that tears run down God's face when his children turn against him and his desires for them. I wonder how our lives would change if we carried with us the image of a brokenhearted, tear-stained Abba Father. Something tells me we'd start making progress in our fight against the pandemic of sin.

THE DAILY QUESTION OF SIN

I'd been talking for quite a while, and Darius was staring off into the distance, his hands folded under his chin. I hoped he was deep in thought and not just bored.

"What are you…," I began.

"You know," he interrupted, "I must have heard a thousand different sermons about sin from my angry pastor when I was growing up. But he never told us we were breaking God's heart. He just told us we were going to hell. He always came across so condemning. Funny, I only thought that sin ticks God off. I never considered that God weeps over my sin."

Darius paused, this time his eyes were downcast as he stared at the floor.

"Man, I know what you're talking about," he said quietly. "I've done the stupid stuff and then braced myself for Pops to tear into me, but instead I'd get that look of disappointment. I always said I'd rather have a beatin' than get that look."

"Why do you think that is?"

"Because when you hurt someone, you see what you did in a different light. It's not just that you did something dumb and they're upset. It's more like you now have a window into their soul. That's rough."

Darius turned and looked me in the eye. He seemed re-energized. Even enthusiastic.

"Okay, explain something to me," he said. "I visited a church not too long ago and decided to attend one of their Bible studies. Sure, the woman who invited me was a big reason I was interested. But I heard they were going to talk about some of the things I'd been wondering about, so I went. Well, right at the end of the meeting, the leader mentioned something about original sin. From what I understand, this pretty much means we're sinful without ever having a choice in the matter. So even if it was possible for me not to sin, I'd still be guilty before God. Is that the deal?"

"Yeah, that's a pretty good summary," I said. "Remember when I talked about how death entered the world through Adam and infected all of us? That's the idea behind original sin. David said he was born in iniquity—sin—and in sin his mother conceived him.[12] Now what's deep about that is that David was reflecting on his adultery with Bathsheba. He dealt not only with the act of sin but also with his nature as a sinful person."

"So David was saying that he sinned because he was a sinner," Darius said.

"You got it, but he wasn't using that as an excuse. It's not like he was denying any personal responsibility. But he was admitting a key point: What we do flows out of who we are. And the reason we sin is because we are born as sinners.

"Let me explain it this way," I continued. "When I first held my eldest child in my arms, it was hard for me to contemplate ever having to discipline him. Well, let's just say that didn't last long. When Quentin was about nine months of age, I distinctly remember him crawling around the house and stopping at an electrical outlet. As he was reaching out to play with it, he turned his head to look at me—an obvious sign that he knew (from previous instruction) that what he wanted to do was wrong. I sternly said, 'No!' and he paused for a moment. Then he promptly began playing with the outlet. It was at that moment when it registered—my child, as cute as he was, is a sinner. And his sinfulness isn't a learned behavior as much as it is his innate disposition."

"If I'm so stained by sin right from the start," Darius asked, "why would a God who is holy and pure want to be with a person like me?"

"It's mind blowing, isn't it?" I said. "Are you familiar with the story of Hosea and Gomer?"

"Yeah, our pastor loved that story. It's where God tells a guy to marry a prostitute, right?"

"Exactly. And God did that because he wanted Hosea to feel what it was like to be jilted by an adulterous woman. It was an illustration of God being rejected by his unfaithful children."

"How's that?"

"Because God equated Israel's sin with unfaithfulness to him. And if you've ever known anyone who's been cheated on, you've obviously encountered a person who has experienced a lot of pain. Which is exactly what we inflict on God when we sin."

Darius got quiet again. It was as if there was something he wanted to say but didn't know how to say it. He was searching for the words.

"Didn't Gomer cheat on Hosea while they were married?"

"Yep."

"And didn't God tell Hosea to take her back?"

"Yep."

"Amazing. I've never been married, but I can assure you two things. One, I would never marry a prostitute; and two, if my wife cheated on me, I would *never* take her back."

"Pretty incredible illustration, isn't it?" I said. "It's really an illustration of God's grace—something he has plenty of. Something he poured out on Israel time and again. Something he has poured out on us plenty of times too."[13]

Just then the attendant came over to tell us they were closing for the night. We grabbed our stuff and headed for the parking lot.

"Hey, I'd like to hear more about what you were saying about God's grace," Darius said. "I've heard about it before, of course. But I'm still not really clear on what it is. Maybe you could come over to my apartment and we could talk about it…over dinner even."

"I'd love to."

THE MAZE OF GRACE

It's Important to Remember Where We've Been

Go now and leave your life of sin.

—JESUS OF NAZARETH (John 8:11)

There is one thing the world cannot do. It cannot offer grace.

—GORDON MACDONALD

Darius and I had arranged to meet at his apartment the following Thursday night. We had planned for an early dinner, and when I got there promptly at six, he was busy in the kitchen.

"Smells good in here, man," I said. "What we got cookin'?"

"Oh, you know, a little red beans and rice, some fried catfish. But I grilled a piece for you, of course." He looked at my stomach with that big smile of his.

"I didn't know you could cook."

"There's a lot of things about me you don't know." For some reason, his smile had disappeared.

As I moved to the living room, I saw several pictures of Darius with an attractive woman.

"Is this your girl—" I started to ask, but just then the door opened and the woman I saw in the pictures walked in. She greeted Darius with a kiss and opened the closet door to hang up her jacket. Darius pointed me out. "Jocelyn, this is the guy I've been telling you about."

"Oh, the pastor?" she said nervously.

"Yeah, 'the pastor,'" I said. We chatted briefly before Jocelyn went to the bedroom to change out of her business suit. When we sat down for dinner, Darius jumped right in.

"Do you think I'm going to hell for living with a woman I'm not married to?" he asked. "I mean, that's pretty much what my mother says."

Jocelyn, uncomfortable with Darius's bluntness, coughed nervously.

"Of course I don't think that," I said. "I mean, you all could just be friendly roommates." It was a weak attempt at humor, but Darius laughed anyway. He probably thought I'd lost my mind.

"I don't think Jocelyn would mind me telling you that we do what most seriously dating couples do," Darius said, as if to dispel any confusion on my part.

With that, Jocelyn left the table to get some coffee. I almost asked if I could help her, since the conversation was getting uncomfortable for me as well. Instead, I just concentrated on eating until she returned.

"Jocelyn, did you grow up going to church?"

"I'm Catholic," she said. "I guess you could say I'm one of those Easter and Christmas Catholics."

"Man, I can't believe I forgot the desert!" Darius interrupted. "Sorry, but I've got to run to the store real quick." He grabbed his keys and left. I was glad to have a chance to talk with Jocelyn without the distractions of Darius's frank admissions. Jocelyn told me about her experience in Catholic school, and how she continued going to Mass and confession during college. But over the last few years, she'd become disillusioned by the hypocrisy she saw in the church, and she found herself drifting from her beliefs.

"I guess that's the common ground Darius and I have," she said. "We both grew up religious, and we still believe in God. We just don't believe that the brand of God we were sold was the right one."

I was feeling more comfortable with our conversation, so I asked Jocelyn a risky question. "How do you feel about living with Darius?"

"I felt real bad about it at first," she said. "It went against everything I was taught growing up. But that's a long story."

"What do you mean?"

"Well, I believe kids get programmed by their parents. You know, we all receive some sort of value system, right or wrong. Well, part of the value system I inherited was the sanctity of marriage, and along with that, a high value on remaining a virgin until you're married. My dad always said, 'Your virginity is a gift that should only be given to the man you marry.' So I was bound to feel guilty regardless of what I did."

"How do you feel about these things now?"

"Do you mean after we have sex?"

Her bluntness startled me. I sipped some coffee, then said, "Yes."

"Well, there is still a twinge of guilt," she said. "Darius was telling me what you said about eternity being written across our hearts, and I see that in this situation. There's always a voice telling me that what I'm doing isn't right, but that voice is starting to fade."

Jocelyn got quiet, then said in almost a whisper, "I don't think I can do enough Hail Marys to be forgiven for the last couple of years."

Just then Darius returned from the store with ice cream. "So what were you guys talking about?"

Looking at Jocelyn, I said, "I was just about to explain God's grace."

With the sun dropping below the Jerusalem horizon, the flames of scattered lanterns begin to light the Palestinian evening. In the twilight a woman tends to a few hurried details as she prepares for something she never thought she'd do.

Before leaving her dwelling, she does a final check. Every strand of hair is neatly pulled back, and she has rubbed fragrant oil on her skin. She then slips outside, but immediately she checks the street. She's taking another big risk, and she must be sure the coast is clear. Did she notice a figure in a doorway down the street? She isn't sure, but still she makes her way down the dusty street, turns east, and continues to walk. Everything in her mind tells her to turn back. What she is doing goes against everything she has been taught since childhood. But somehow her heart keeps her feet moving.

Finally she arrives. The man is waiting, at the home of a friend. His wife is home with their children. When the woman slips inside, she immediately reaches for his warm embrace.

What follows is an evening of sin—adultery in its most classic sense.

Hours later, still in darkness, she knows she should return to her family. But she and her lover have pressed their luck enough times in the past that they take another risk. Their adulterous relationship has become too comfortable, so they linger there.

Did she hear a sound outside? She shakes her lover awake. He sees her sitting up, clutching the covers to her chest.

"I know you're in there," a voice announces from the other side of the door. "We're coming in!"

The next thing she knows, she's being dragged out of the house by a group of men more fearsome than Roman soldiers. They are Pharisees, bent on enforcing the Mosaic Law against adultery.

Forced to sit alone in the dirty street, she sees the religious gestapo gathering stones. She knows she will die by being stoned to death. Filled with regret, but knowing well the law against adultery, she braces herself for the pain of broken bones, the bleeding, and the eventual death.

"Hey, I've got an idea," one of the Pharisees says to his comrades.

"Jesus is in town. You know, the self-proclaimed Messiah. He acts like he knows everything, so let's see what he says about this one."

"I hear he'll be teaching at the Temple," says another. "Let's take her there."

The trembling woman is granted a temporary reprieve.

The Pharisees take their time dragging the woman into the Temple courts, to prolong her humiliation. A crowd has gathered to hear from the rabbi named Jesus. He begins teaching on the Kingdom of God but loses the crowd's attention. They have turned their eyes to the band of Pharisees dragging a young woman into the Temple. They force her to her feet and thrust her into the presence of Jesus.

Mockingly, one of them says, "Teacher, this woman was caught in the act of adultery. In the Law Moses commanded us to stone such women. Now what do you say?"[1]

The woman is in tears, and Jesus is quiet. He's concentrating not on the woman, but on the men who brought her here. Their hands already hold the stones for her execution. Without saying a word, Jesus squats and begins writing with his finger on the dusty ground. What he writes is barely visible to the bystanders, but the Pharisees see it clearly. He stands up, looks directly at them, and says, "If any one of you is without sin, let him be the first to throw a stone at her."[2] The Pharisees are dumbfounded. Jesus then goes back to writing in the dust. One by one the accusers leave.

The woman is trembling, knowing that she narrowly escaped death but not knowing what the rabbi will do next. Does a worse fate now await her?

"Woman, where are they? Has no one condemned you?" Jesus asks.

"No one, sir," she says.

"Then neither do I condemn you," Jesus declares. "Go now and leave your life of sin."[3] The woman deserved death; instead she found grace.

The peculiar thing about this woman—and this story—is that we don't know much about her. We don't know her name, what she looked like, how old she was, or how long she'd been sleeping with another woman's husband. We don't even know if she heeded the words of Jesus and put a stop to the adultery. All we know is that she committed adultery, was caught, deserved death according to Old Testament law, but instead found grace from Jesus. I guess that's all that really matters.

But something tells me there's more to the story.

A lot has been made over what Jesus scribbled in the dust. I would love to believe that he wrote out the sinful deeds of the Pharisees who had condemned the woman. I can see him looking each Pharisee in the eye, jotting down a secret "indiscretion," and smiling as the Pharisee lowered his head in awe and shame, wondering, *How did he know that?* While this is merely speculation, we do know that whatever he wrote was powerful enough to strip the Pharisees of their self-righteousness, causing them to drop their stones and leave the Temple.

What is often missed from this story is that the woman was not the only one who bumped into grace that day. With a few words etched into the dirt, Jesus let it be known that the woman caught in adultery and the Pharisees were all in the same boat—everyone was in need of grace. And if justice was to be exacted equitably, she wasn't going to be the only one punished.

The message of this story is clear: Everyone needs grace! But something leads me to believe that the woman deserving of the scarlet letter was the only one who really got the message that day.

WHERE OUR HEALING IS FOUND

The Pharisees were so consumed with punishing sin that they missed the bigger picture. Like present-day prosecutors who build their cases on the letter of the law, the Pharisees missed what was most important. They failed to realize that the Law exposes sin; it doesn't heal it.

What heals is grace.

This is the bigger picture that often gets missed: Jesus did not come to condemn, but to heal. He came to reform sin-stained sinners, *all* of us. And what reforms us is his grace.

Matthew Poncelet's childhood was one that far too many people can identify with. His father was an alcoholic who died when Matthew was only twelve, leaving him to cope with life without a male presence. He was one of four sons his mother had to raise alone—a seemingly impossible task. Sure enough, Matthew took a turn for the worse.

That worse turn came when he and Carl Vitello raped a young woman several times, then killed her and her boyfriend. Matthew was eventually caught, tried, and sentenced to die by lethal injection in the state of Louisiana. Some were irate that he was sentenced to die. Most, however, were relieved. And all refused to reach out to him.

Except Sister Helen Prejean.

This kindhearted and devoted nun befriended the hardened criminal, a man who prided himself on being a white supremacist and a follower of Hitler's Nazi ideology. Through great acts of courage and kindness, Sister Prejean acted as an instrument of grace. She was able to soften the heart of this man whom many considered to be more animal than human. And before Matthew Poncelet was injected with poison that would inflame his lungs and stop his heart, he was touched deeply by grace.[4]

The debate over capital punishment continues to rage. Is this really the best means of justice? Is there a better way? Back and forth the arguments go. But while there's a definite place for justice—no matter what that looks like—there must also be a preeminent place for grace.

John the apostle saw justice as well as grace in the life of Jesus. Not only did John see "the Word," which "became flesh and made his dwelling among us," but John said that when he beheld the incarnate Jesus, he saw a man "full of grace and truth."[5]

And this is the great paradox of Jesus Christ. Contrary to what some think, he did not come to eradicate the Law. His commitment to justice is seen in his instructions to pay taxes, respect the house of God, and submit to the laws of Caesar. He was indeed a man full of truth.

But he was also a man full of grace. He allowed a woman who had been bleeding for years to touch him publicly, contrary to the custom of that day. He refused to shun a prostitute who was "erotically" (as some would say) letting her hair fall to her shoulders and wiping his feet in public, to the ire of the Pharisees. And he ate freely with those considered to be the biggest sinners of that day. His grace so permeated his life and ministry that he was dubbed the "friend of…'sinners.'"[6]

He was a man full of grace *and* truth.

I struggle with labels. People sometimes want to know if I am a conservative or a liberal. Am I a Baptist or a Presbyterian? Do I believe in God's complete sovereignty or in humanity's free will? I normally respond by discussing where I fall on the issues and then conclude by saying I am a follower of Jesus Christ. Labels, like words, evolve over time, and they come with different sets of presuppositions. Some people say liberals don't honor the full authority of Scripture. And they say that conservative evangelical Christians, right or wrong, are the keepers of the Law, that they overflow with truth but are deficient in grace.

This point is emphasized every time a minister "falls into sin," most often in sexual immorality. Conservative Christians are faithful in the justice department and remove him from the pulpit. Yet I have seen hardly any cases where the process was also full of grace. Churches seem to be great at sending a pastor's family to the unemployment line but poor at helping to heal what was infected. What heals is grace.

Left to the judgment of many conservative Christians today, Peter the apostle would be looking for a job selling cars, because he had the audacity to deny Jesus Christ. Paul would never have made it into ministry because he persecuted Christians for so long. And Jesus? Some of our conservative brethren would keep him away from their pulpits because of his associations with less-than-noble people such as the prostitute and the tax collector Zacchaeus.

No wonder so many churches have turned into glorified country clubs filled with people who have little spiritual impact on society. Too many Christians have mastered the art of picking up stones and killing their own and, in the process, have forgotten how to heal. And what heals is grace.

The movie *Les Misérables* illustrates beautifully the medicating power of grace. As the film begins, Jean Valjean has been released from prison and is the picture of desperation. Seeing his condition, a bishop invites Valjean into his home for dinner, and while they eat, Valjean eyes the silverware, thinking of a way to steal it. Sure enough, in the middle of the night Valjean takes off with the bishop's precious silver.

The next morning the police bring Valjean back to the bishop's home, confident that the clergyman will press charges. But instead, the bishop reminds Valjean that he had forgotten to take the candlesticks with him when he left.[7]

This act of grace forces the police to release Valjean. Now free, Jean Valjean is a transformed man who deals graciously with everyone in his path, even his archenemy. What changed him? In a word: *grace*.

THE SPIRIT OF THE SACRED NARRATIVE

Grace is a refreshing wind that blows throughout the pages of the sacred narrative. Grace is not something that abruptly appeared on the scene when the incarnate Christ stepped out of heaven and onto earth. Grace was around long before that.

I grew up in the church. And from those early flannel-board days, I picked up on the idea that the Old Testament represents law, while the

New Testament represents grace. This message was nailed down when I went to seminary, where professors characterized the Old Testament as the age of the Law, while much of the New Testament and our current era they labeled the dispensation of grace.

But such a view overlooks an amazing record of God dispensing his grace throughout the Old Testament. The early books of the Bible are not simply filled with archaic laws set down to condemn sin. Far more is in these books than instances of God's judgment in demanding that nations be destroyed or the meticulous rules addressing such minutiae as what to do when a woman is experiencing her menstrual cycle.

It's easy to read such passages and conclude that the Old Testament is irrelevant. But in coming to this conclusion, we fail to see that God has always been a God of grace. It's not only his nature, but it's a theme beautifully woven throughout the sacred narrative—from the start.

God's undeserved favor is seen most clearly against the backdrop of sin. Like a jeweler who displays a beautiful diamond against a dark velvet cloth, God's grace becomes clear when we see it against the contrasting bleakness of our sin.

When Adam and Eve should have been killed on the spot for their rebellious decision to disobey God, his mercy and grace stepped in. When Lot should have been destroyed with the rest of Sodom and Gomorrah, God's grace showed up. When David should have died for his acts of adultery and murder, God graciously gave him another child through Bathsheba. And when Israel abandoned God for the umpteenth time, God graciously allowed the people to come back to him.

When God decided to create a nation from the descendents of Abraham, he did it so that all people of the earth would be blessed.[8] Ever since then, God has been working out his plan to offer salvation to a dying world and to create a people for himself—the heirs of grace. His plan has been unfolding since the beginning of time, and it continues today.

THE MAZE OF GRACE

Two statements ring true: First, we all need reformation, and second, none of us is capable of reforming ourselves. The pandemic of sin has wreaked havoc on every aspect of creation and humanity, meaning that we're all dysfunctional messes. Our sinfulness has driven a wedge between us and God. Consequently, the one thing we deserve is an eternity separated from him.

But God refuses to give up on us. He loves us too much to lose us without doing everything he can to draw us to himself. We are marred by sin, but we can still commune with the eternal, holy God. This is totally an act of love and grace on God's part. And it is amazing.

Random House Webster's College Dictionary defines *amaze* as "causing great wonder, astonishment; to bewilder," and even to "perplex." That's an apt description of God's grace toward us.

John Newton, a former slave trader, wrote:

Amazing grace! how sweet the sound,
That saved a wretch like me!
I once was lost, but now am found;
Was blind, but now I see.[9]

No doubt inspired by these words of John Newton, Stuart Townsend, in his song "How Deep the Father's Love for Us," similarly describes humanity as "wretches."[10] And herein lies the amazement: A holy God, stretching out his hand to sinful wretches, calls us to sit on Abba's lap, adopting us as his children.

But herein also is our great spiritual struggle. We see ourselves as anything but wretches. Like the Pharisees, we readily condemn others because they lack our level of "righteousness"—which we feel we've been instrumental in acquiring. It's too easy to justify ourselves and condemn everyone else and, in the process, miss the point that we desperately need God's grace.

When it comes to grace, we have more Pharisee in us than we have Jesus. We easily forget who we are and where we've been.

In his book *What's So Amazing About Grace?* Philip Yancey tells the story of a prostitute who was selling her two-year-old daughter to men for depraved sex. The mother could make more money in one hour by doing this than she could make herself in an entire night of work. When she was asked by Yancey's friend if she wanted to go to church, she declared, "Church! Why would I ever go there? I was already feeling terrible about myself. They'd make me feel worse."[11]

Sadly, she's right.

In a lot of ways I can identify with a story I heard several years ago about a preacher who had an unusual gift—a gift for preaching. It was evident that he was destined to accomplish great things for God. When he was in his early twenties, he began preaching across Europe. Initially the venues were small churches, but before long his preaching expanded to vast open spaces, where thousands would come to listen. At the end of a sermon, he would extend an invitation, and the altar would be flooded with wretches wanting to experience God's grace.

Yet this preacher was a closet alcoholic—a public success and a private failure. When he could no longer stand the duplicity, he stopped preaching and disappeared from public view. The next several years found him in various taverns, stumbling nightly in a drunken stupor. The booze led to other things, and he never knew whose bed he might find himself in.

Then the light shone.

One morning the now middle-aged man awoke and sensed as never before the presence of God urging him to leave his sin behind. Immediately he left the booze and the women and wandered into an Anglican church. Sunday after Sunday he would sit in the back and feel the tender touches of grace as God began to reform the wretch that he was.

He once again started preaching, and slowly the crowds began to come back. Then it happened…

He was in one of England's largest churches. The house was packed, and the choir had begun its final song. The preacher was going over his thoughts, preparing to take his place behind the pulpit, when an usher slipped him a note.

Scribbled across the paper were words that caused the man's heart to race. It was a note from a woman he had shamefully used for sexual pleasure. It read, "Hardly anyone here remembers you.… They have no clue who you really are, the alcohol and the sex. But I know. And I intend to expose you the moment you get up to preach, to let the whole world know the sinful wretch that you are!"

Tears trickled down the anxious preacher's face. He was finished.

When the choir's song ended, he moved to the podium. The crowd was hushed, waiting to hear his eloquent sermon. But instead of eloquence, they got something they never expected.

"I was just handed a note by a woman. A woman from my past. A woman I shamefully committed immorality with years ago. She's here tonight, and she says that she plans on exposing me for who I really am, a sinful wretch. And everything she says about me is right. I know you didn't come to hear a sinful wretch. You came to hear a preacher. But before I am anything else, I am a sinner who has unexplainably bumped into the grace of God.… I had a message planned tonight and was going to make an altar call for people to come experience the grace of God. But if you'll forgive me, I need to be at the altar this evening. Because I've forgotten who I really am—a sinner saved by grace."

With those words he moved to the altar. It was dead quiet in the packed church—an awkward kind of quiet—as this man stood in tears amazed at God's grace. And slowly, one by one, men and women, boys and girls came desperately to the altar to join him. There, thousands of wretches lingered, basking in the grace of God.

I know exactly what that preacher meant. I'm a husband, a father, a pastor, and a preacher. But before I'm any of those things, I am a wretch who has been saved solely by God's grace.

I turned to Darius and Jocelyn. "It would be hypocritical for me to condemn you for living together," I said. "I haven't forgotten what I was and where I came from before I encountered God's grace. It makes me miserable just to think of the mess I was caught up in. But grace is what freed me."

They looked at each other for a moment, and it seemed that Jocelyn had tears in her eyes. The silence was starting to grow louder.

"I'm going to head home," I said. "It's getting late."

Jocelyn and Darius walked me to the door. I gave Jocelyn a hug, and Darius shook my hand. Then he leaned forward and whispered, "Thanks, man. You gave us a whole lot to think about."

I drove home wondering what it was they were thinking.

THE NORMAL LIFE

What You See Is Not All There Is

Upon that cross of Jesus Mine eye at times can see
The very dying form of One Who suffered there for me;
And from my smitten heart with tears, Two wonders I confess—
The wonders of His glorious love And my own worthlessness.

—Elizabeth C. Clephane, "Beneath the Cross of Jesus"

You were bought at a price.

—Paul the apostle (1 Corinthians 6:20)

Okay, I know that what Jocelyn and I do is 'wrong,'" Darius said. "But in our world it doesn't feel wrong because it's normal."

We'd been standing on the shore of a lake not far from my church. I picked up a stone, and as I skipped it across the water, I said, "Yeah, I know what you're saying. And what makes this even more difficult for you is that you're wrestling with your faith. If you weren't looking for a spirituality that rings true, living with your girlfriend wouldn't even be an issue."

"That's right," he said, as he skipped a rock of his own.

"If I can move past this surface issue and go a little deeper, I think what's most difficult for you is thinking about things you'd have to give up if you got serious about following Jesus. In a weird sort of way, I think that's what is confining you."

"What do you mean?"

"It seems like you have this weird view that Christianity is about giving up things, the things you enjoy the most. If that were true—if that were the effect Christianity had on our lives—then I wouldn't be drawn to it either."

Smiling, Darius said, "Well you know where I got that view of Christianity from."

"Let me guess, your old pastor?"

We laughed as we skipped a couple more stones across the surface of the lake. Then I turned to Darius and said, "What you learned in church is not the normal Christian life."

She's gone. And she didn't have the decency to say good-bye.

At first he thought she just went out to run an errand. But it's been days now, and his panic has peaked. He's racked his brain searching for an explanation for her abrupt departure. Was it something he said? Did he express disappointment with her? Or maybe it was because he always left his shoes lying in the middle of the family room. He could hear her repeated complaint: "It's not just the shoes; it's the fact that I'm trying to keep a clean house, and you don't respect my hard work enough to put them away." But surely she wouldn't leave over a pair of sandals?

He moves quickly through town, frantically asking friends, acquaintances, and strangers if they've seen his wife. No one has.

In the heat of the day, he rests at the town's well to gather his thoughts and cool off with a drink of water. As he sits he thinks back to their wedding day. He smiles at the thought of what had to be the weirdest day in his life.

First, there was the odd assortment of wedding guests. There were his wife's old boyfriends, who couldn't believe she was getting married. And her family—talk about strange! He smiles even now at the memory. But the smile disappears when he thinks about the people who were missing. Much of his own family refused to come. The thought of his marrying an openly adulterous woman was appalling. Especially when you consider that he was in the ministry. How could he do such a thing? To this day there is tension in the extended family over his poor choice of a wife. His father barely speaks to him. His mother comes by, but infrequently, and only to see the grandchildren. But he's not angry. How could he be? From their perspective, marrying this woman did seem to be a bad decision.

But they didn't know that he had no choice in the matter. God told him to marry her. And there was no question that it was God speaking. The Lord even gave him a reason: Marrying an adulterous woman will illustrate God's relationship with Israel. And so he married her...reluctantly.

Immediately he was the talk of the town and the entire nation. He was declared guilty in the court of public opinion. This was just no way for a prophet to behave.

It's just after noon, and he has had no success in finding his runaway wife. Though he's tired, he's relieved at the same time. She's gone. That's a good thing, right? A divorce will be readily given, his name and ministry will be restored, and he can get on with life.

Just as he's about to leave the well, a caravan passes by. It's making its way to the market, where it will sell its human cargo to the highest bidders. He sees her just as the last of the horses passes by. She's bound by chains, headed for the center of town to be sold. At the last moment their eyes meet, and then she coldly turns her head.

Those eyes, that look, reveal a woman who has never been in love with him. She gave him everything but her heart.

As he stands and stares at the thinning cloud of dust, he's convinced that the relationship is over. In a few moments she'll be the property of yet another man who will lease her body to lusting customers who will use her over and over. He's through with her. How he ever agreed to marry her in the first place was an act of God.

He kicks a pebble as he makes his way toward home. And then he hears it—it's that same voice.

"Hosea."

Why does the voice always come at the most awkward moments?

"Yes, God."

"Go, show your love to your wife again, though she is loved by another and is an adulteress. Love her as the LORD loves the Israelites, though they turn to other gods and love the sacred raisin cakes."[1]

He obeys the voice and takes his seat amid the diverse crowd that's gathered at the market. Sitting just behind him are several wealthy men. They wear the finest of robes and are adorned with lavish rings. To his left and right are other men from a lower class. Their missing teeth are obvious as they begin to pant over the women who come up for sale. The thought of his wife being enslaved to one of these men causes Hosea to move uneasily forward in his seat.

The man presiding over the auction bangs his gavel, letting everyone know the day's business has begun. The first woman is presented to this motley crew. It's her…Gomer.

The frigid eyes that earlier in the day had brushed off her husband have now softened. They reveal a sense of fear, and it melts his heart.

Before anyone else can offer a bid, Hosea stands up and declares, "I'll buy her back. This woman is my wife."

The auctioneer responds, "Well, you're well aware of the Law. The Law requires a redemption price of thirty shekels."

Hosea checks his pocket. He has only half the required price.

"I only have fifteen shekels, sir. But I also have about a homer and a lethek of barley."

"Fair enough," the auctioneer responds. "She's all yours."

Gomer's chains are loosened, and Hosea embraces her. Then, placing his hands squarely on either side of her soft cheeks, he says, "You are to live with me many days; you must not be a prostitute or be intimate with any man, and I will live with you."[2]

With tear-filled eyes Gomer nods in agreement. She has been redeemed.

BREAKING THE CHAINS

"Darius, I'm guessing that you heard the word *redeemed* over and over in church when you were growing up. We used to sing hymns that declared this wonderful doctrine every Sunday morning. But like so many other words that are used in church, I never really understood what it meant."

"Yeah, the choir at my church used to sing an anthem that kept repeating that word—redeemed, redeemed, redeemed. It could almost hypnotize you," Darius said. "It was never one of my favorite songs."

"Well, the song might not have impressed you, but the theme of redemption in the sacred narrative could easily become a personal favorite," I said. "When someone understands this teaching, it's hard to resist."

The concept of redemption in Scripture has to do with buying something back. It carries with it the idea of releasing someone from bondage. Think about these verses from the sacred narrative:

> In him we have redemption through his blood, the forgiveness of sins, in accordance with the riches of God's grace.[3]

For all have sinned and fall short of the glory of God, and are
justified freely by his grace through the redemption that came
by Christ Jesus.[4]

For he has rescued us from the dominion of darkness and
brought us into the kingdom of the Son he loves, in whom
we have redemption, the forgiveness of sins.[5]

The incredible release, the redemption that we can experience
through Christ, is presented against the background of bondage. To be
redeemed, you first have to experience bondage, since being released
assumes that at one point you were bound. Paul the apostle described the
contrast between bondage and redemption, saying we are rescued from
"the dominion of darkness."

The pandemic of sin affects us all, keeping us locked in the realm of
darkness. Sin acts as a jailer, preventing people from experiencing the
quality of life God intended. People think they know how to live, but
they go about their daily lives without realizing they're in prison.

Our culture tends to factor God out of the equation, elevating pleasure and self-fulfillment as the highest goals in life. Those who focus on
pleasure consider the redeemed folks to be the incarcerated ones, since
they are prevented from enjoying the "real" pleasures of life. In our culture's eyes, those who have been set free by God are actually held captive
to religious traditions and restrictive beliefs. That's why Billy Joel poked
fun at a Catholic girl named Virginia in one of his songs.[6] He was trying
to get in bed with her, but she was resisting his attempts at seduction.
Some people admit that religion might have value in their lives at some
future time. But right now, they're just having too much fun to get serious about the life of faith.

There's nothing wrong with pleasure as long as God is a part of it,
but people who try to find the meaning of life in pleasure are deceived.

Those things that look like fun are really the chains of bondage. Sadly, people don't know they're marching to the orders of the world's jailer: Satan, the Deceiver.

DECEPTION AND SPIRITUAL BONDAGE

Satan's deceitfulness began in the Garden of Eden, when he convinced Eve to eat the fruit that God had declared off-limits. And man, was there a price to pay! Adam and Eve were kicked out of the garden, they experienced the curse of God, and—most tragically—sin entered the world. All because Eve was convinced that she hadn't been experiencing life to the max. Along came the Deceiver who lied to her about what she was missing, and she fell for it.[7]

I went shopping once at a store in Los Angeles. I was drawn to this store because they had really great-looking clothes, but none of them had price tags. *No problem,* I thought as I walked to the cash register. *They couldn't be* that *expensive.* When the cashier had finished ringing up my merchandise, I was in shock. The shirts were beyond expensive! Embarrassed, I told her to take them back, and I apologized for wasting her time.

As I drove home I realized there were no price tags because of guys like me. Normally when I go shopping, the first thing I look at is the price. But I couldn't do that when there were no price tags. I was drawn to the clothes because of how beautiful they were, so I decided to ignore the likelihood that they were too expensive. As the cashier was ringing up the total, I thought that even if it did go over my budget, I'd still get the shirts. But when the cost was announced, I had to choose between the clothes and my marriage!

No doubt that store has caught many others through the same ploy. Enticed by the beauty, many ignore the cost. And that's how the Deceiver works. He appeals to our senses first by showing us that beautiful woman, that once-in-a-lifetime moneymaking scheme, or that enticing drug or drink. He never—and I mean never—shows us the cost. He hides the price tags of divorce, sinful addictions, and unethical actions, and we grab the merchandise. But at some point we have to pay up. There are billions in our world who, like Edmund in *The Lion, the Witch and the Wardrobe,* are bound by the appealing but addictive chains of Turkish Delight.[8]

WEARING THE CHAINS

Look around and you'll see that most people are wearing chains, and I don't mean cool gold chains. So many people are chained in the bondage of the world's system—the pursuit of pleasure and possessions and wealth—that it blinds them to their bondage. People don't even realize there's an alternative.

One of my favorite movies is *The Shawshank Redemption.* The film depicts life in prison over a span of several decades. One of the inmates has spent more of his life behind bars than he has in the outside world. When he's finally released, he has to adjust to living in a world that has progressed beyond his wildest imagination. In a telling scene he is almost run over by a car, something he'd never seen before. Unable to cope with the transition to normal life, he finally hangs himself.

The former inmate had grown too accustomed to the routine of prison life. And at some point the routine became safe. It defined life for him. He didn't have to worry about earning money or finding his next meal. He didn't have to worry about being run over by a car or paying bills. He enjoyed a certain level of comfort when he lived behind bars. Prison life was safe, and for him it became "normal." Prison blinded him to real life, the life that goes on outside prison walls.[9]

That's how it is for a lot of us. Life in chains fits our definition of "normal." It's normal to be immoral as long as it brings pleasure. It's normal to lie when it's to our advantage. It's normal to cheat on our tax returns. It's normal to be rude and to slander people. After all, they need to know we can't be stepped on. Bondage to the world's system is the rule, not the exception. And sadly, the fact that just about everyone else is bound in chains has blinded people to the bondage they are in. They don't even notice it.

It's sort of like an American who visits a primitive village in a Third World nation. The visitor is shocked at the sight of people living in thatch-roofed huts with mud floors, gathering grubworms, and cooking tree bark for a meal. But all of these things seem completely normal to the villagers. And just as an American would be shocked by the tribe's cultural norms, the tribesmen would be equally shocked if they visited a neighborhood in Chicago or Los Angeles. *What's the deal with all the different hair colors and the smooth skin?* the villager might wonder. *And why is everyone wearing those uncomfortable clay-colored trousers? They could easily just go without.* We are the odd ones in their minds.

THE CURVE

"Yeah, I can see that who's 'odd' depends on which person is making the judgment," Darius said. "But are you saying that customs are so ingrained that when I go out and party with my friends, I'm not really choosing to do those things? I'm really just doing what the system tells me to do? If that's what you're saying, I don't buy it. If I'm with Jocelyn, for instance, it's because I *want* to be with her, not because someone is making me do it."

"You're right," I said. "You *are* choosing to do these things. But while you're doing what you do, you think that's what life is all about. Just hangin' out and havin' fun. You don't see how the world's system dictates what you do and how you define life.

"That was the essential problem people had with Jesus. When he came to earth to offer people redemption from their chains, he had to first convince them that the chains existed. Although life back then was normal according to the world's definition, it wasn't the life God had intended for people. When Jesus exposed people's sinfulness—things they considered nothing more than cultural norms—not only was he rejected, he was ridiculed as being the odd one.

"It got so bad that a leading faction within the religious leadership started plotting ways to take Jesus's life. In their minds, he was like that annoying smart kid in grade school. When I was in school and blew a test, I used to ask the other kids how they thought they'd done. I was glad when they thought they'd blown it, because that meant the teacher would grade on a curve and it would make all of us look better even though we'd all done poorly.

"But there was always that one kid who was the know-it-all. He'd ace the exam and ruin the curve. I found myself wanting to take him somewhere private and beat the daylights out of him. That kid wrecked the curve for the rest of us.

"That's why the Pharisees got so mad at Jesus. Prior to his coming, they saw themselves as the standard of righteousness. But then Jesus came along with a new, perfect standard that exposed the chains that bound the Pharisees and everyone else. Jesus not only upset the cultural norm, he totally wrecked the curve by gracefully demonstrating what the normal, abundant life God intends for us looks like. He wrecked the curve by showing that life is not meant to be lived in chains. And he's offered us the keys that lead to our release from bondage."

"I can tell you one thing," Darius said. "You're doing a fine job of wrecking *my* day."

The Longing of the Soul

All of humanity is blinded to their chains, myself included. It's easy for a life lived outside of God's plan to become normal. We just accept it. But there is also a subtle awareness that our souls are in prison. There is an innate uneasiness about life, even though we often can't put our finger on just what it is. I believe the nagging feeling we have that there must be more to life is directly related to occasional glimpses of our chains.

Think about the human tendency to build altars. It's an attempt to satisfy the longing of the soul. Whether it's the altar of Materialism or Rationalism or Pleasure or Relativism, we've been trying to find the key that will release our souls from bondage. All of this and more points to the discomfort we experience—a discomfort that comes directly from the glimpses we have of our chains. Our souls become exasperated with their prolonged imprisonment.

Getting back to *The Shawshank Redemption* for just a moment: The longing of our souls is a close parallel to Andy Dufresne's experience as he enters the prison. As he is abused by some of the men and shunned by others, his frustration grows. Then he catches a break when he gets to use his gifts as an accountant in a job for the warden.

During his time in the warden's office, a new inmate comes to Shawshank, and through a strange set of circumstances he tells Andy that he knew of a guy who admitted to murdering Andy's wife and her lover. Excited that his name could now be cleared, Andy goes to the warden—who promptly turns him away. Andy vents his frustration, which lands him in solitary confinement.

When he is finally released from "the hole," Andy longs as never before to taste life outside the prison. Andy's longing leads him on a quest that takes decades to achieve, a quest that becomes his passion, as he quietly digs an escape tunnel in his cell during the long nights. Here was a man who was acutely aware of the unnaturalness of his surroundings and who refused to be satisfied with a life in chains.

One night Andy finishes the tunnel, and he makes his escape. The next day, when the warden discovers that Andy is missing, he's furious. In frustration he throws a stone at a large poster in Andy's cell, discovering a hole where the wall should have been.[10]

And so it is with us. The alarm clock of our souls has awakened our longing to be released from our chains. Most of us, like Andy, spend our lives digging for our redemption. We dig by trying to be "good people." We dig by trying different religions. We dig by trying to do more good things than bad. But the sacred narrative tells us that we don't have to dig our own escape route. The key that unlocks our chains is within reach. It's useless to seek our own escape in anything outside of Jesus Christ. Trying on our own will only leave us incarcerated. And if we die in bondage in this life, it doesn't bode well for the afterlife.

The basic message of the sacred narrative is that life bound by the chains of sin is not the life God intended for us. To take pleasure in our incarceration is not only tragic, it's foolish. Especially when you consider that God has provided our escape route, with the winds of freedom awaiting us outside.

chapter ten

LIFE ON THE OUTSIDE

Pursuing Your Soul's Craving for Freedom

It is for freedom that Christ has set us free. Stand firm, then, and do not let yourselves be burdened again by a yoke of slavery.

—PAUL THE APOSTLE (Galatians 5:1)

I have come that they may have life, and have it to the full.

—JESUS OF NAZARETH (John 10:10)

Jocelyn was out of town on business, and Darius had invited me to his place to watch *Roots* on video. We'd spent the last several hours witnessing the violent history of slavery in the United States.

"This movie always gets me!" Darius said. He was angry, on his feet, pacing the floor. "I mean, if I had lived back then, I would have bashed somebody's head in."

"No you wouldn't have," I said. "As a slave you would have picked that cotton just like everybody else."

Darius didn't want to give in that easily, but he finally had to agree. "I guess since all I've known is freedom, the only reaction I have when I see something like this is anger."

"Try rage," I said.

"It's just so hard to imagine that was how things really were. And for the most part, blacks and whites accepted it. I mean, you got used to someone always talking down to you and abusing you."

"Freedom really does spoil us," I said.

"Yes it does," he agreed.

"For me, that's what's really interesting about this movie. I see so many parallels between slavery and Christianity."

"Why doesn't that surprise me?" Darius said with a smile.

It was one of the ugliest chapters in America's past. The economic prosperity of our country was built on the backs of slaves. Men and women were sold into slavery from the shores of West Africa, packed onto ships, transported through the Middle Passage, and sold again in America to the highest bidders.

And their next stop didn't provide a reprieve.

Life on the plantations was inhumane, whether the slaves were toiling on rice plantations in South Carolina or cotton fields in Mississippi. The women often fell victim to rape, as "massah" would leave his wife in the big house to embrace barbaric pleasure in the slave quarters. The offspring of such assaults had it no easier, as they were caught between two worlds. They were scorned by other slaves for thinking they were better than everybody else, and they were hated by white society for being "niggers." Ironically, untold numbers of slaveholders' children lived as slaves.

When the life of slavery became unbearable, many decided to steal away up north, risking their lives in search of freedom. Many didn't make it. Hunted by dogs as if they were animals, escapees were beaten, bound, and taken back to the plantations. Sometimes limbs were cut off, and on extreme occasions, slaves were killed. All of this was done publicly to teach the rest of the slave population a lesson: Whoever tried to escape would meet the same fate.

Then Abraham Lincoln issued his famous Emancipation Proclamation, announcing freedom for the enslaved. Yet as powerful as Lincoln's words were that January day in 1863, ultimately they did not end the institution of slavery. First, a war had to be won. And finally, with the eventual ratification of the Thirteenth Amendment, slavery was officially ended and a new life was promised for a whole race of people. A life outside the plantation—for most.

Yet this moment in history would reveal a great irony. In my mind's eye I see slaves shouting with joy at the news of their eventual freedom. But I also see many of them, perhaps most, wondering what in the world they would do when that day finally came. They were eager to live in freedom, but never having been free, how could they suddenly embrace a life of freedom?

For years all that these men and women had known was the plantation. It defined the boundaries of their lives. It was their place of community, where they shared some semblance of life together. Then at the end of the Civil War, with the Southern states defeated, the slaves were free to leave. But where would they go?

Almost all of them were illiterate. Few had received significant training in a trade, and while they had honed basic skills in manual labor, most didn't know how to handle money. All this and more stacked the odds against their finding success in the outside world, which led many to remain within the familiar confines of the plantation.

These men and women had been emancipated, set free to determine their own destinies. But ironically, many refused their freedom and chose to stay on the inside—at the plantation. They chose a place that was known for bondage instead of embracing the freedom that was theirs for the taking.

Not much has changed today. Our emancipation from the chains of sin was provided on a hill called Calvary in ancient Palestine. Through the death of Christ, we were redeemed and emancipated. And within each person who comes to Christ and accepts his gift of salvation, there's something that cries out in joy over the gift of freedom. But sadly, while we've been set free, most of us still choose to hang around the plantation of sin, ensnared in its chains and living without hope. Many never really experience what it's like to live life on the outside.

THE NECESSITY OF DEATH

It's a paradox, but the sacred narrative tells us that a prerequisite for living the normal Christian life, the life of freedom on the outside, is death.

> For we know that our old self was crucified with him so that the body of sin might be done away with, that we should no longer be slaves to sin—because anyone who has died has been freed from sin.... In the same way, count yourselves dead to sin but alive to God in Christ Jesus.[1]

> If by the Spirit you put to death the misdeeds of the body, you will live.[2]

> Put to death, therefore, whatever belongs to your earthly nature: sexual immorality, impurity, lust, evil desires and greed, which is idolatry. Because of these, the wrath of God is coming. You used to walk in these ways, in the life you once lived.[3]

God's instructions about death as the crucial element to being free to enjoy life on the outside can be confusing. On the one hand he tells us that when we come to faith in Christ, our old self (our sin nature) is put to death. But then he turns around and tells us to put it to death, implying that it's still alive. So what is it: dead or alive?

This paradoxical nature of sin is heightened when you consider that the verses cited above come from the apostle Paul. Paul tells us in the book of Romans that sin has been put to death through Christ, but then in chapter 7 he cries out, "What a wretched man I am! Who will rescue me from this body of death."[4]

Paul uses an interesting word picture—"body of death"—to help us understand sin. In Roman culture, when someone was found guilty of murder, one of the potential punishments was to chain the murderer to the decaying, stinking corpse of the murder victim. Everyone who saw this person could easily identify him as a murderer.

With that image in mind, Paul equates sin to a decaying, stinking corpse that he can't seem to shake loose. This is the point of his frustration: Even when he wants to live in freedom, he still finds the corpse of sin chained to his body.

When Jesus died on the cross, old man sin was killed once and for all. He was taken off our backs so we could experience life in Christ on the outside, in total freedom. But there's a problem. Just as many of the slaves in the American South chose to stay on the plantation, far too many Christians find themselves willfully living under the corpse of sin, refusing to take it off their lives. We've been set free, but we choose to live in bondage to sin. This makes no sense, but here's at least part of the explanation: Humans gravitate toward what's easy and comfortable, such as the familiar patterns we've established. The slaves who were granted freedom but chose to stay on the plantation did so because plantation life, though brutal at times, was what they were used to.

While our spiritual emancipation provides the opportunity to live life the way God intended—in absolute freedom—there's a constant temptation to go back to what is comfortable. The attraction of sin is powerful and unavoidable. The only way for our backs to be relieved of the rotting corpse is to consider ourselves dead to sin. The sacred narrative teaches us that in order to live, we must die.

In the book *The Color of Water,* a biracial son pays tribute to his Jewish mother, Ruth Shilsky, who migrated with her family from Europe to Norfolk, Virginia, when she was young. Learning a new language and getting used to new customs were just two of the many transitions she had to make. One new custom was getting used to life in the segregated South of the 1930s.

Norfolk's racial divide was clearly defined. As Ruth settled into a part-time job, helping run the family convenience store, she tragically crossed the racial divide. She fell in love with an African American friend and eventually she got pregnant by him. Ruth's mother quietly sent her to live with relatives in New York. Her Jewish relatives, unwilling to deal with a baby of African American descent, rushed her to a doctor who performed an abortion.

While Ruth's family was successful in killing the baby, they failed to kill Ruth's desire to be with black men. She eventually married an African American man. Ruth tried to hide her marriage from her family, but when they got wind of it, they held a funeral service for their still-living relative.

Thinking back on that time, Ruth tells her son, "My family mourned me when I married your father. They said kaddish and sat shiva. That's how Orthodox Jews mourn their dead. They say prayers, turn their mirrors down, sit on boxes for seven days, and cover their heads."[5]

Ruth's family considered her dead when she was obviously moving around and breathing, which is a dramatic picture of what it takes to live on the outside, set free from the bondage of sin. The sacred narrative instructs us to consider ourselves dead to sin. Just as Ruth's family acted dead toward her, even though she was still living, we're to consider ourselves dead to sin, even though the temptation to indulge our sin nature feels very much alive.

TORN BETWEEN TWO WORLDS

My little boy has a dilemma. He loves to run outside and play in the backyard. He loves to jump on the slide and play in his fort. But he hates playing by himself. Normally I go out and play with him, but at times I can't. I watch him run out the door toward the slide, and as he runs, he looks over his shoulder at me as if to say, "I'd really love for you to be here with me." He gets on the slide, and I return to my work. But within a few seconds, he's back inside, begging me to come outside. I tell him I can't, and he goes back out. And the cycle continues: back inside, then back outside. He's stuck. He really wants to be outside, but he also really wants to be with me. And so he tries to enjoy both worlds but gets frustrated when he discovers that in his quest to enjoy both, he has enjoyed neither.

That was me back in high school. I was trying to make the Christian faith my own and was beginning to fall in love with God. But I also craved the acceptance and approval of my friends who didn't share my passion for Christ. Like my son, I was torn between two worlds.

My attempts to please my friends led me to do things such as standing out on the corner after football games drinking Old English 800— "eight ball" we called it. One night I got drunk with my friends and then tried to talk to them about Christ. It just wasn't working.

I was going in two directions at the same time until Cedric, one of my drinking partners, sobered me up. We were sitting in art class, and I was trying to share Christ with him. Right in the middle of my plea for him to give his life to Christ, he put his hands in the air and lowered his head, begging me to stop. His next words still ring in my head.

"Bryan, how in the world are you going to convince me to be a Christian? You do the same things I do. The only difference between us seems to be that when you sin, you have a guilty conscience and I don't. If all your religion can offer me is a guilty conscience, then I don't want it!"

Cedric had identified the futility of trying to live on the plantation and on the outside at the same time. We can enjoy the life God intended for us only when we die to our former life and our inclination to return to the plantation of sin.

This is what Jesus was talking about when three men were given the chance to live on the outside, in the freedom of following Christ. All three let the opportunity pass by because they were unwilling to die to plantation life. When the final man tried to cut a deal with Jesus that would allow him to revisit the other path first, Jesus told him: "No one who puts his hand to the plow and looks back is fit for service in the kingdom of God."[6] In essence, Jesus was saying that if you and I want to live life on the outside, we must choose to never go back to the life of slavery to sin.

This scene baffles me. Jesus has what amounts to three people wanting to join his "church." Not only does he not allow them to join on their terms—and if you study the passage, you'll see that their terms aren't that unreasonable—but he doesn't even try to sway them by highlighting the benefits of following him. He just gives a few terse words and lets them go on their way.

Jesus was no high-pressure salesman. He was not consumed with appealing to people's felt needs. To him, living in freedom was an either/or proposition, take it or leave it. In fact, when it came to "selling" people on the life of freedom, Jesus went out of his way to point out the difficulties. Consider what he told his disciples:

> I am sending you out like sheep among wolves. Therefore be as shrewd as snakes and as innocent as doves.
>
> Be on your guard against men; they will hand you over to the local councils and flog you in their synagogues....
>
> All men will hate you because of me, but he who stands firm to the end will be saved....

Do not suppose that I have come to bring peace to the earth.
I did not come to bring peace, but a sword. For I have come to
turn "a man against his father, a daughter against her mother, a
daughter-in-law against her mother-in-law—a man's enemies will
be the members of his own household."

Anyone who loves his father or mother more than me is not
worthy of me; anyone who loves his son or daughter more than
me is not worthy of me; and anyone who does not take his cross
and follow me is not worthy of me. Whoever finds his life will
lose it, and whoever loses his life for my sake will find it.[7]

Sadly, most who were sent out that day didn't "make the cut." Life
on the outside proved too rough of an adjustment from the comfortable
chains of the plantation. And so back they went.

There's a moving episode in the life of the apostle Peter that never
fails to stop me in my tracks. Jesus has died and Peter is trying to sort
through what appears to be a shattered, wasted life. He's spent the last
three years following this controversial rabbi only to blow it now by
deserting and even betraying him. With his life in pieces, Peter decides to
go back to what he did before Christ came along: fishing.

Going back to his former occupation is far more than a mere job
change for Peter; it represents a bewildered man throwing up his hands
and going back into bondage. As he sits on that boat, catching nothing,
he wonders what's next. His wife will be glad to have him around more.
He'll probably go back to the synagogue. Go back to the old friends. Go
back to his former way of life.

A frustrated smile appears on his face as he looks at the empty net that
he and his partners just pulled in. No fish—a gentle reminder that he was
never very good at this. For a moment he lets his mind wander back to
the day he met Jesus. That day he was in the same situation—working
hard but catching no fish. He remembers the awe he experienced when

this rabbi, this novice of a fisherman, told Peter and his friends to cast out one more time. Before they knew what was happening, their nets filled with fish. In fact, they caught so many fish that their boat began to sink. He thinks, *It sure would be nice to have Jesus around now to tell us where to cast our nets.*

Just then a man on the beach shouts, "Don't you have any fish?"—a frustrating question for men who had been out all night fishing and have nothing to show for their efforts.

"No," they yell back.

"Tell you what. Why don't you throw your net on the right side of the boat, and you'll find something."

The men aren't too far from shore, and they're ready to call it a day. But what can one more cast hurt? So they cast the net exactly where the stranger tells them to. And when they bring in the net, there are so many fish in it they can't haul it in. They'd seen this before. It has to be Jesus!

Peter dives in the water and swims to shore while the others make their way in for a rendezvous with Jesus.

After a delicious fish fry on shore, Peter begins to lose his excitement. He feels the uneasiness in the air. He had betrayed and deserted Jesus before the crucifixion. Surely Jesus wants nothing more to do with him. He glances at Jesus, whose eyes seem to burn a hole in Peter's heart.

"Peter, do you love me?"

What a question!

"Yes, Lord."

"Feed my lambs."

Peter lets his eyes drop, but Jesus stays focused on him.

"Peter, do you *really* love me?"

Just when Peter thinks his heart can sink no lower, it does. Why does Jesus keep asking this question?

"Yes, Lord, you know I do."

"Take care of my sheep."

Peter keeps his head down.

"Peter do you *really* love me?"

Crushed to the depths of his spirit, Peter again replies, "Yes, Lord, you know everything. You *know* that I love you!"[8]

Peter hurts because for the first time he recognizes just how deeply his actions had wounded Jesus. He hurts because Jesus's gentle call for him to "feed my [Jesus's] sheep" reminds him that just a few hours earlier, he had ventured back onto the plantation and was now being called out again into freedom.

Peter faces a choice: He can do what's comfortable on the plantation or step outside into freedom and "catch men."

Jesus doesn't make the choice any easier. He wants Peter to think seriously about what it will cost him to live on the outside. Jesus says, "I tell you the truth, when you were younger you dressed yourself and went where you wanted; but when you are old you will stretch out your hands, and someone else will dress you and lead you where you do not want to go."[9]

Think about what that means. To say it another way: "Peter, life on the outside will eventually cost you your life! You will die because of me!" Finally, after saying these words, Jesus, the consummate salesman, says to Peter, "Follow me!"[10]

"Consummate salesman?" Darius said, laughing. "Jesus sure wouldn't cut it in sales today! He never makes any of this stuff sound appealing."

"You're right," I said, "because he wants us to take seriously the choice that's in front of us. But that isn't to say there aren't tremendous benefits to living the life of faith. Life on the outside will make you a better man and, at some point, a better husband, and it will give you peace you won't find any other way. Those are legitimate benefits, and things that God wants us to experience and enjoy. But putting too much emphasis on the benefits has resulted in a Christian culture that has grown soft because we've diluted the gospel message. We've offered easy benefits that supposedly come from following Christ. The truth is, following Christ is never easy. And it's never primarily about meeting our needs or desires.

"Life on the outside offers no promises of success or temporal well-being. If you venture outside, you may lose your job. You may lose friends. You may even lose your life."

"If that's the case, then what's the payoff?" Darius asked.

"I hesitate to try to answer that," I said. "I could give you a list of things that will sound good, both the short-term and the long-term benefits. But maybe another time. Right now, if I were to mention just one reward for venturing out to live in freedom, it would be the word *destiny*.

"You and I were not created in God's image so we could live in slavery. We were created to live in freedom, experiencing our God-ordained purpose and destiny. A huge part of our destiny is to live freely in union with God and to glorify him with our lives. Our souls crave the freedom that only life in fellowship with God can give us."

Abraham Lincoln's Emancipation Proclamation announced the eventual liberation of the slaves from physical bondage to the white man. But long after the end of the Civil War, they remained in social bondage. Their new slave master was the system of segregation known as Jim Crow.

They couldn't use certain public restrooms, water fountains, or hotels. They had to sit in the back of buses and were barred from lunch counters. No matter how long they waited in certain stores, if a white customer came in, they got pushed aside. This was daily life in the "emancipated" South for a century.

Until Dr. Martin Luther King Jr. showed up.

Dr. King had caught a glimpse of what life on the outside looked like for his African American brothers and sisters. He dreamed of a day when men would be judged by who they were on the inside, not by what they looked like on the outside. He dreamed of a day when children of different colors and ethnicities would at last be truly free.[11]

His glimpse of life on the outside led him to the front lines of marches. It landed him in jail. And the vision of life lived on the outside sent him to an early grave. But along the way he inspired a generation of African Americans to seek their own destinies, to experience the longings of their soul—freedom—and to accept nothing less.

Dr. King followed the example of Jesus Christ. Jesus saw the status quo—our bondage to sin—and refused to accept it. Taking the position of authority at a synagogue one Sabbath, Jesus unrolled the scroll of the prophet Isaiah and declared these words about himself: "The Spirit of the Lord is on me, because he has anointed me to preach good news to the poor. He has sent me to proclaim freedom for the prisoners."[12]

Jesus's journey to free the prisoners would lead him to confront Pharisees, heal hemorrhaging women, and hang out with prostitutes and tax collectors and other notorious sinners. And it would ultimately lead to his early, but necessary, death—so that you and I could enjoy the freedom that only life on the outside can provide.

chapter eleven

MEMPHIS WINDS

Preparing for Two Unavoidable Appointments

When you die they might have a jury trial to decide whether you're going to heaven or hell.... But I think they'll say, "Well, he's the only one who can play like that; we better let him in."

—MILES DAVIS

For as the lightning comes from the east and flashes to the west, so also will the coming of the Son of Man be.

—JESUS OF NAZARETH (Matthew 24:27, NKJV)

T hat's what I want," Darius said. "I want a life of freedom, mean-ing, and destiny."

We were still at his apartment, still talking after we watched *Roots*.

"I want so bad to experience the freedom that God brings, but I don't know if I'm ready to really die like you talked about. I just don't know."

I could relate to his frustration.

"I know it's hard," I said. "And I know the dilemma you're in." I turned over a junk-mail envelope that was lying on his coffee table and drew a line with a solid circle at one end and an arrow at the other.

"You're right here," I said, as I added a dot in the middle of the line. "This line represents your life. The small circle at this end is your beginning, and the arrow at the other end represents eternity, your life after you die."

Then, looking at Darius, I said, "What you're dealing with right now will have a profound impact on your future. That's not to say you'll never have another chance to change your destiny. But all we're really promised in this life is the present moment. Tomorrow is never guaranteed."

It was early on a Tuesday in July when I hopped into my Honda Accord to drive to a little restaurant on the corner of Park and White Station in Memphis. I was going to have breakfast with a member of our church, a man I knew very little about. His name is Andrew Smith.

We arrived at the diner at the same time. As he hopped out of his pickup, I noticed he was carrying a thick book, a thick history book to be exact.

"Don't think I'm a nerd," he said. "But I need to take some time after our meeting to brush up on my history."

During our meal he explained that he had taken a job as a history teacher at a local classical school.

"A *classical* school?" I asked.

"Yeah, it's a private school where the students learn Latin and Greek early in the education process."

As he shared some about his educational journey, it became clear that Andrew was no intellectual lightweight. He planned on getting a second master's degree in philosophy, and he had a love for theology.

Our conversation took several turns, from books we had read to Andrew's interest in the theological foundations of the church I pastor.

The more we talked, the more I appreciated Andrew, and the more excited I got that he was part of our church.

And then it happened.

As I was sharing my passion for our church, I noticed that he kept looking outside. I found his short attention span to be a little unsettling. Okay, so some hard rain was coming down, but anyone who's spent any time in the Mid-South knows sudden showers are nothing unusual. A day that you think will be perfect—the type where you blow the day off playing eighteen holes of golf—ends up having a ten-minute, out-of-the-blue thunderstorm. And just as quickly as it comes, it goes.

Surely Andrew knew this being a native Memphian. So why was he constantly peering outside? I continued talking, trying to ignore the rattling of the bread carts in the nearby storage room. Then I realized the rattling had nothing to do with bread carts.

Stopping midsentence to look outside, I saw a torrential downpour coupled with extreme winds. The lights flickered, and people in the parking lot were running back to their cars. Medium-size trees were twisting violently. Andrew and I sat silently in fearful awe.

And just like that, it was over.

My cell phone rang, and my wife nervously asked if I was okay. She had heard a tremendous force hit our home, so she'd gathered our sleeping boys in the safest place in our house and was waiting for the storm to end. I hurriedly told Andrew good-bye and headed home. As I neared our neighborhood, I noticed telephone poles snapped in two. The road was partially blocked by century-old trees that had been uprooted. Some had crushed cars with the weight of their fall.

As I drove down our street, my heart raced. A tree had caved in the roof of one neighbor's home, and another huge tree had fallen in the middle of a church cemetery. Pulling up to our house, I saw what my wife had heard. Our next-door neighbor's tree had crashed down into our yard, taking out her fence, our gate, and several power lines, and had narrowly missed our car. The tips of its branches had brushed against our home, knocking loose some of our siding and ripping out the electrical box.

Ninety-mile-per-hour "straight-line" winds did the damage, born out of three separate meteorological conditions that had come together over Memphis. Many declared it a once-in-a-lifetime event. But as unique as this event was, the experiences of Memphians over the next several weeks were not unique.

The Memphis Winds that visited us early on that Tuesday morning caused a drastic change of lifestyle for more than three hundred thousand people. Few people had power. For well over two weeks, there was no air conditioning. No checking of e-mail. No dishwashers running. No washing machines. No television.

The regular routine of life was gone, all in a span of thirty minutes. The storm touched some families more deeply than others. Four people died, one a seventeen-month-old baby. As the power outage wore on, people left their homes to stay with friends or relatives. With the mass exodus came mass break-ins, as criminals took advantage of the vacated homes. Most businesses, including banks and grocery stores, were closed. Other residents were frustrated when their weekly round of golf or a trip to the movies had to be canceled. I talked to one elderly couple who had lived in their home for more than six decades. When they first moved in, they planted a tree, and now, sixty-three years later, that strong tree was lying across their front lawn.

The Memphis Winds could not have happened at a worse time. If you've ever been to Memphis in the teeth of summer, you know that air conditioning is a necessity, not a luxury. The few hotels that did have power suddenly found themselves to be the most popular places on earth.

Our family called more than twenty hotels before finding one with a vacancy. The next several weeks, we lived in hotels, eating out every meal and desperately longing for a return to life as we knew it. Our sense of desperation was a theme shared by the entire community. People just wanted to get back to some semblance of a normal life. A life they took for granted prior to the Memphis Winds.

THE UNEXPECTEDNESS OF LIFE

Forrest Gump was familiar with the unexpectedness of life. "Life is like a box of chocolates," he noted. "You never know what you're gonna get."[1] Just when he thought life was going one way, all of a sudden it whipped him around in the opposite direction. Just when life was hitting a groove going upward, it yanked him downward.

But James, the brother of Jesus, would have disagreed with Gump's assessment of the unexpectedness of life. In so many words, James said there are a few pieces of candy that are always in life's proverbial candy box, and they're called trials. James tells us not to be surprised, and in fact to "consider it pure joy" when we "face trials of many kinds."[2]

James didn't say *if* we face trials, but *whenever* we face trials. They're a natural part of the terrain of life's journey. We should expect the unfortunate, unplanned-for events that attack us. Life will continue to hit us with Memphis Winds.

A grandmother gets Alzheimer's. A son is paralyzed after a collision with another player on the football field. A friend battles cancer. A co-worker goes through a nasty divorce. The stock market drops. A deacon loses his job. A wife has to deal with an alcoholic husband. A teenage daughter finds out she's pregnant. Your car breaks down again, and you don't have the money to get it repaired. All of a sudden, life as you've always known it is radically changed.

The sacred narrative tells us that as long as we're leasing time on God's green earth, these winds will come. They are impossible to plan for and impossible to predict. But there will always be those once-in-a-lifetime occurrences that will change life as we know it. We should expect it.

THE WINDS OF DEATH

I'm not a doomsday prophet, but the sobering reality of the winds that wreaked havoc on Memphis that July was a reminder of how little control we have and how fragile life is. We might think we have a firm grip on life's steering wheel, but at the end of the day, we're just lucky to be along for the ride.

Death is a constant reminder of this truth because it's the consummate expression of our lack of control. The writer of the book of Hebrews gives us this sober reminder: "It is appointed unto men once to die, but after this the judgment."[3]

We all have two inescapable appointments, and the first is with death. Unless Christ returns first, we all will die. Eat as healthy as you like. Jog as much as you want. Lift as many weights as possible. None of this will prevent death. Death is as much a part of everyone's journey as life is. For some it looms just around the corner; for others it remains off in the distance. But it gets here eventually.

The great irony of death is that everyone knows it's coming, but few of us prepare for it. Sure, we buy life insurance, make out a will, and handle our finances knowing that someday, hopefully in the far distant future, we will die. Yet far too many of us don't *really* prepare for death.

And after death, we will all fulfill our second and final appointment: standing in the presence of God to give an account for our lives. He won't ask if our life-insurance policy is adequate to provide for the loved ones we left behind. He won't bother asking about a will or whether we ate a healthy diet. We will stand in front of our Maker, beholding his glory, and we'll have to answer for the way we handled our lives for the few moments we spent on earth.

The only way to really prepare for death is by living on earth in full awareness of the reality of God. This is the urgent message James was trying to convey in the sacred narrative. He was ticked at the wealthy folks who assumed that life was their big oyster, and who wrote all of their plans in ink as if they could guarantee the outcome. Desperately trying to get them to see the fragility of life, James begged:

> Now listen, you who say, "Today or tomorrow we will go to this or that city, spend a year there, carry on business and make money." Why, you do not even know what will happen tomorrow. What is your life? You are a mist that appears for a little while and then vanishes. Instead, you ought to say, "If it is the Lord's will, we will live and do this or that."[4]

James used the image of a mist to depict the brevity of life. Like a mist, life appears and then it vanishes. Life moves incredibly fast. Too fast.

"Wait a minute. Why the sudden dark turn?" Darius asked. "We were talking about life and its meaning. We were talking about freedom from bondage and God favoring the little guy. Now all of a sudden you're on this death kick. What gives?"

"We can't live life in the freedom of God and his grace unless we also understand the meaning of death and judgment," I said. "It's not something any of us likes to think about, but it's necessary.

"Maybe this story will explain some things. As a kid I couldn't wait until I got to high school where I'd have my own locker and start changing classes every hour. Well that day came and went. Then I couldn't wait until high-school graduation when I'd get a car and head off to college. That day came and went. Then I couldn't wait to graduate from college, start making money, and get married. Check that off the list. Next up was starting a family. Let's see, I have two kids.

"It's funny that when you're a kid, you can't wait for your next birthday. (Remember you used to tell people, 'I'm five and a half'?) Now as adults we're holding tightly to the reins of life, begging for it to slow down, trying desperately to hold on to the fleeting mist that is our life. Never before have so many people spent so much money getting face-lifts and tummy tucks and hair implants, trying to fight off the effects of aging. These are desperate but futile attempts to slow down the passage of time, to extend our years on earth.

"Nothing we do will add a day to our lives. We're just whistling past the graveyard. Our appointment with death and our meeting with God are coming. So there is a definite need to make sure that when we stand in the presence of God, we are prepared for that appointment."[5]

Not long after that storm left Memphis without electricity and basic services, I sent my wife and two sons to Chicago to stay with relatives. I didn't go because I had to speak in Iowa that Monday, so I endured a couple of incredibly hot evenings in our powerless home.

It felt like ninety degrees that evening as I tried desperately to fall asleep. I opened windows and threw off blankets but was still having trouble. My frustration only mounted when I heard a disturbing buzz from across the street. Around midnight I checked out where the noise was coming from. The whole street was dark except for one home. Several of his lights were on!

The next morning I went over there. Suppressing my frustration, I told him that I noticed he had power.

"Yeah, I bought a generator during all that Y2K stuff a few years ago," he said. "My wife said I was spending money on something we wouldn't need. We didn't need it back then, but thank God we have it now. You're welcome to come over and enjoy the air conditioning and watch a little television anytime you want."

I thanked him as I left the coolness of his home. I thought about how handy a generator would be. As I tried to get to sleep again that evening, listening to the less-than-soothing buzz of my neighbor's generator, I promised myself that I would invest in a generator the next day.

Most of us take life for granted, just as I'd always taken electricity for granted. Polls tell us that most people believe in life after death, but few *really prepare* for it. When death comes, they aren't ready.

When I was growing up, preachers used talk of death as a scare tactic to get people to think about the condition of their souls. But death is not really a scare tactic; it's just a reality that we'll all encounter. We need to prepare for the meeting with God that comes after we die. I'm not suggesting that we simply say a quick prayer that will hopefully keep us out of hell. Instead, we need to live our lives in submission to God and in a relationship with him. We need to live in light of the truth that our lives are nothing more than mist—here one moment and gone the next. The only way we'll make the most of our brief time on earth is to surrender our lives fully to God.

Miles Davis thought he was making the most of his time on earth by playing his trumpet and living life according to his own rules. He was so convinced of this that he once remarked that when he died he would stand outside heaven's gates playing his trumpet and that God would have no other choice but to let him in. Eminem's Academy Award–winning song "Lose Yourself" proposed that the way he made the most of his life was by losing himself in the music.

But they're both wrong. The point of the sacred narrative is that creating great art or doing good things or getting more religious is not enough. You have to realize that the brief time you've been granted on earth comes from God. Your life has been given to you not to live according to your own plans, but according to God's plans and purposes for you.

We're all sinful creatures, which means that without God, we have no hope. There is no way on our own that we can live lives that please God or bring him glory. We have to rely on him, not on our own efforts. We have to confess that we need him and invite his Spirit to come into our lives, filling our lives and guiding us into God's truth. The Holy Spirit empowers us to overcome sin in our life journey. That's our hope.

LIFE AFTER DEATH

Death is a morbid subject to many, but there's another way to look at it. For those who are God's children, physical death is the beginning of a new life. God gives meaning to our lives on earth, as short as they are. Then he gives us meaning in the next life as we enjoy his presence and give him glory for eternity. We prepare in this life for the next life by walking with God our Father. God wants us to walk with him through life, like a child walking with his daddy. It's a journey we take, and at times we'll veer off the path. At other times we'll be so worn out that we'll want to give up. But we've got to keep moving by drawing on God's strength. The life of freedom is not an easy journey, but in the end there's nothing more fulfilling, because we'll be accomplishing our destiny. And when we die and stand in God's presence, we'll be ready for our appointment with him, because we've spent our lives walking with him.

Several years ago I went to Augusta National to watch a practice round of the Masters, one of the most prestigious tournaments in all of golf. For about seven holes I fought through crowds to catch a glimpse of Tiger Woods working his magic. I watched him hit high fading shots onto treacherous greens. I stood in awe as he blasted three-hundred-yard drives down narrow fairways.

I also saw him do something very strange. I first noticed it on the greens. The other golfers would aim their putts at the hole. But not Tiger. When he made it to a green, he had his caddy put down a tee on some obscure place on the green, and for several minutes Tiger would putt over and over again, aiming at that tee, and then he'd move on.

Then there were the tee shots and the approaches. On a par-three hole, the other guys in Tiger's group hit high, beautiful shots that landed near the pin. When Tiger took aim, he hit a high shot to the back right of the green, about fifty feet from the pin. I heard his caddy say, "Great shot, Tiger." I turned to the gentleman next to me and said, "Great shot? That doesn't look so great to me." But the man saw something I had missed.

"I know it didn't seem great," he said, "but Tiger wasn't aiming for the pin. He was aiming for where the pin will most likely be placed on Sunday."

Sunday's pin placements are traditionally the toughest. Tucked away in some difficult place on the green, they require the most precise shots. Because of this, tournaments are won or lost on Sunday. In the practice round, Tiger wasn't preparing for where the pins were placed that day. He was looking ahead, concentrating on Sunday's game. While the other golfers were content to play in the present, Tiger was playing for the future.

In the sacred narrative, James tries to prepare us for life's realities. He tells us about the unpredictable Memphis Winds, which are unexpected but always guaranteed. They're unavoidable reminders for us to stop playing merely in the present and to play with Sunday—eternity—in mind. When we encounter things we can't control, we are reminded that we don't really control anything. It's all up to God.

This is the only way we can successfully navigate the journey of life. The sacred narrative reminds us to stop aiming at the pin placements of earth and to aim instead at where God has placed the pins—with eternal meaning and significance in mind. When we do that, we'll be ready for our appointment with God.

Darius bowed his head, looking at his knees and drumming his thumbs together. I knew this was his habit when the wheels were turning inside.

"Do you think I'm a Christian?" he asked.

"What a question! What makes you ask?"

"All this stuff we've been talking about has made me question whether I am or not. I mean, I said 'the prayer' when I was four years old. But based on what we've been talking about, I really don't see a lot of change in my life, or much to indicate that I'm a follower of Christ. You know what I mean?"

"Sure."

Finally, Darius pointed to a Bible lying on the coffee table.

"The stuff in this book, this 'sacred narrative' as you call it, really hasn't jumped off the page into my life," he said. "And all of that makes me wonder: If my life were to end right now, would I be ready?"

"Darius, you mentioned saying 'the prayer' when you were little. I have a problem with Christians who put pressure on people to remember the exact moment when they said the prayer and invited Christ into their life. I don't think what we're talking about has so much to do with a point in time. It's more a process, a journey that we take in life. I mean, look at our relationship. How long have we been hanging out now?"

"I don't know, several months maybe?"

"Right. And the Darius I met in that little diner several months ago is not the same Darius I know today. Without realizing it, you've already begun the journey. You've started 'dating God.'"

That got his attention. "What do you mean, 'dating God'?" he asked.

"You know how dating is all about checking somebody out. It's great. You talk on the phone, go out to eat, do a lot of stuff together, but with no real commitment. You don't have to give up much. You're just getting to know each other to see what it might lead to. But marriage, on the other hand, is a whole different story."

"You're telling me," Darius said. "All my boys who got married can't hang out like they used to."

"Exactly, because marriage demands giving up some things in order to obtain certain things. Marriage is a serious commitment. So serious, in fact, that the sacred narrative describes it as a covenant."

"A covenant?"

"Yeah. The narrative talks about all types of covenants, and the common denominator with covenants is sacrifice. That's why virginity was such a big deal back then. In some cultures it was so significant that when a couple got married, the parents would check out the bedsheets after the wedding night. If there was no blood, then the woman would be killed because it was assumed she wasn't a virgin. The marriage covenant, like other ancient covenants, had to be confirmed by the shedding of blood.

"And that's how it is with our relationship with God. The covenant that God made with us demanded that someone's blood be shed. And that was Jesus Christ. When you decide to stop dating God and move into a covenant of commitment to him, he seals that covenant by the blood of his Son, Jesus. So the big question is, When are you ready to stop dating God and enter into a covenant relationship with him? Because dating him isn't enough."

Darius was quiet, thinking about all this.

"I guess I'm ready to experience this destiny thing you talked about earlier," he said. "I really want to experience the kind of life God wants for me, whatever that may bring. Dating God was cool, but it's not enough. I'm ready for a covenant commitment to God."

I left Darius's apartment feeling happier than I had in a long time. But I was also worried for Darius. He had to face a lot of things as he started out in his new relationship with God. What would happen with him and Jocelyn? How would she feel about the commitment he had just made? And how would Darius make the shift from finding his identity in women, friends, and possessions to finding his identity as a beloved child of God? And what about his friends who might not welcome all the changes in his life?

Just then, God interrupted me. It was as if he said, "I think I can handle this."

The next morning I arrived late at my office at the church. It had been a long night. And on top of that, I couldn't sleep when I got home. I was so excited for Darius.

I booted up my computer and found an e-mail from Darius's mom:

Last night Darius called us for the first time in months. It was so late when he called that we thought something was wrong, and we feared the worst. (We really do worry over our boy.) But instead of getting bad news, we got the best news a parent could ever get. I think the best way to say it is in Darius's own words: "I've decided to stop dating God and accept his invitation for marriage." I'm one of those old fundamentalists, and it took me awhile to figure out what my son was talking about. I'm still not completely sure, but I guess all of this means he is going to be a lot more serious about his relationship with God. Whatever you said, the Lord used you. I couldn't be happier.

Madeline

P.S.: My sister Olivia has a son about Darius's age who could use a little help. I'll call and schedule an appointment for him to come see you.

I couldn't stop laughing…

NOTES

Prologue

1. Darius—as well as his views and comments—is a composite of many of the twenty-something people I've conversed with over the past few years. His beliefs reflect a common questioning of the church and the Bible.

Chapter 1

1. Michael Jackson, "Living with Michael Jackson," interview by Martin Bashir, *20/20*, ABC, February 6, 2003.
2. Wayne A. Grudem, *Systematic Theology* (Grand Rapids: Zondervan, 1994), 267.
3. Galatians 4:4.
4. John 1:14.
5. Galatians 4:6.
6. Job 12:10.
7. Acts 17:28.
8. To read the complete story about the reluctant prophet who shirked his duty, was swallowed by a giant fish, and later was regurgitated onto the beach, read the book of Jonah in the Old Testament. It's a short book and worth the read.

Chapter 2

1. Thomas Hauser, *Muhammad Ali: His Life and Times* (New York: Simon & Schuster, Touchstone, 1991), 18.
2. See Genesis 12:1-3.
3. John 1:46.
4. Isaiah 6:3.

5. See R. C. Sproul, *The Holiness of God* (Wheaton, IL: Tyndale, 1998), 38.
6. See, for example, John 3:11, NASB.
7. Psalm 51:5.
8. Romans 3:23.
9. Romans 3:10-12.
10. John Newton, "Amazing Grace," *The Broadman Hymnal* (Nashville: Broadman Press, 1940).

Chapter 3

1. Malcolm X, *The Autobiography of Malcolm X* (New York: Ballantine Books, 1964), 226.
2. Malcolm X, *The Autobiography of Malcolm X*, 227.
3. *Malcolm X*, directed by Spike Lee (Burbank, CA: Warner Brothers, 1992). The movie is based on *The Autobiography of Malcolm X*.
4. To read these stories in greater detail, see Exodus 3; 13:17-22; 14; 19–20; 33:12-23.
5. To read Rahab's story in more detail, see Joshua 2; 5:13–6:27.
6. See Hebrews 11:31; see also Matthew 1:5.
7. 1 Corinthians 15:9.
8. Ephesians 3:8.
9. The Judaizers were Jews who taught that in order to be saved, one had to observe certain aspects of the Jewish Law, such as circumcision and ceremonial practices. To read about the Judaizers in more detail, see Acts 15:1 and the New Testament book of Galatians, which was written to refute their teaching.
10. Luke 7:47.

Chapter 4

1. The biggest news story of 1938 is no exaggeration. According to Laura Hillenbrand, author of *Seabiscuit: An American Legend*, that fact is taken from the number of newspaper-column inches devoted to the racehorse

as compared to other major news stories that year. See Laura Hillenbrand, *Seabiscuit: An American Legend* (New York: Ballantine, 2001), ix.
2. Hillenbrand, *Seabiscuit,* 100.
3. Hillenbrand, *Seabiscuit,* xx.
4. To read more about these underdogs, see 1 Samuel 17 (David vs.
    Goliath); 1 Kings 18:16-46 (Elijah vs. the prophets of Baal); and
    2 Corinthians 10 (Paul setting sail on a missionary journey but
    disrespected by the Christians in Corinth).
5. See Genesis 12:1-3.
6. See Exodus 2:1-10.
7. To read about the ten plagues God brought against Egypt, see Exodus
    7–11.
8. To read more about Israel's clamoring for an earthly king, see 1 Samuel 8.
9. To read about Saul's failures as king of Israel, see 1 Samuel 10–15.
10. To read about the selection of David as king of Israel, see 1 Samuel
    16:1-13.
11. To read about David and Goliath, see 1 Samuel 17.
12. To read about this phase of David's life, see 1 Samuel 18–27.
13. Isaiah 53:2.
14. See Joel B. Green, *The Gospel of Luke* (Grand Rapids: Eerdmans,
    1997), 310.
15. To read about this woman, see Luke 7:36-47.
16. To read the story of Jesus and Zacchaeus, see Luke 19:1-10.
17. See Luke 5:30.
18. John 8:11, NKJV.
19. Matthew 23:27.
20. See Luke 21:1-4.
21. See Matthew 6:1-18.
22. See Mark 9:33-35.
23. Matthew 18:3.
24. Matthew 19:13-15.

25. 2 Corinthians 12:7.
26. 2 Corinthians 12:7-9.
27. James 4:10.
28. Bob Geldof, quoted in Paul Williams, *Mother Teresa* (Indianapolis: Alpha, 2002), 191. Emphasis added.

Chapter 5

1. Ecclesiastes 3:11.
2. Tupac Shakur, "I Wonder If Heaven Got a Ghetto," copyright © 1997, Interscope Records.
3. See Luke 5:1-10.
4. Matthew 4:19.
5. Read about Levi in Luke 5:27-29.
6. Read about Solomon's life in the book of Ecclesiastes and in 1 Kings 3–11.
7. See Barry Kernfeld, ed., *The New Grove Dictionary of Jazz* (New York: Oxford University Press, 2003), www.pbs.org/jazz/biography/artist_id_holiday_billie.htm.
8. See Mark 10:17-22.
9. 2 Timothy 4:6-7.
10. See 1 Peter 2:11.
11. See Matthew 6:19-20,33.
12. See Ecclesiastes 12:13.
13. Kernfeld, *The New Grove Dictionary of Jazz*, www.pbs.org/jazz/biography/artist_id_holiday_billie.htm.

Chapter 6

1. *Chariots of Fire*, directed by Hugh Hudson (Burbank, CA: Warner Brothers, 1981).
2. Psalm 29:1-2.
3. Romans 11:36.

4. 1 Corinthians 10:31.

5. See James 4:6; 1 Peter 5:5.

6. See Proverbs 6:16-19.

7. See Genesis 3:4-6 and Isaiah 14:13-15.

8. For more on the meaning of self-giving love, read 1 Corinthians 13.

9. Psalm 21:13.

10. Psalm 22:22.

11. Matthew 8:2.

12. Matthew 8:3.

13. Mark 1:45.

14. *Rocky III,* directed by Sylvester Stallone (Los Angeles: MGM, 1982).

Chapter 7

1. Molly Billings, "The Influenza Pandemic of 1918," June 1997, www.stanford.edu/group/virus/uda.

2. Deseret News, "On the Eve of Peace in WWI Influenza Cast Shadow of Death," www.desnews.com, in Billings, "The Influenza Pandemic of 1918."

3. *New York Times,* May 7, 2003.

4. Romans 5:12.

5. Jimmy Franks, "The Bad Touch," copyright © 1999, The Bloodhound Gang.

6. Proverbs 6:16-19.

7. Proverbs 8:13.

8. Jeremiah 44:4-6.

9. Examples of God's drastic response to certain sins include the following: When an Israelite named Achan sinned against God and his fellow countrymen by taking some of the treasure of Jericho and hiding it, both he and his family were killed (Joshua 6–7). When King Nebuchadnezzar acted in pride and arrogance, refusing to acknowledge God as the source

of his success, he lost his sanity and was driven from his kingdom for seven years, where he lived as a wild animal until he acknowledged God as the Most High (Daniel 2–4). In the New Testament, Ananias and Sapphira, a husband and wife who lied about giving all the proceeds of a land sale to the church, were killed instantly for their sins (Acts 5). A man in the Corinthian church, who was having sexual relations with his stepmother, was removed from the church (1 Corinthians 5).

10. Wayne Grudem, *Systematic Theology* (Grand Rapids: Zondervan, 1994), 490.

11. Read the complete story of the prodigal son in Luke 15:11-32.

12. See Psalm 51:5.

13. Read about Hosea and Gomer in Hosea 1–3.

Chapter 8

1. John 8:4-5.

2. John 8:7.

3. John 8:10-11.

4. *Dead Man Walking,* directed by Tim Robbins (Los Angeles: MGM, 1995).

5. John 1:14.

6. Luke 7:34.

7. Victor Hugo, *Les Misérables,* trans. Norman Denny (New York: Penguin Books, 1982), 104-111.

8. See Genesis 12:1-3.

9. John Newton, "Amazing Grace," *The Broadman Hymnal* (Nashville: Broadman Press, 1940).

10. Stuart Townsend, "How Deep the Father's Love for Us," copyright © 1995 Kingsway's Thankyou Music.

11. Philip Yancey, *What's So Amazing About Grace?* (Grand Rapids: Zondervan, 1997), 11.

Chapter 9

1. Hosea 3:1.
2. Hosea 3:3.
3. Ephesians 1:7.
4. Romans 3:23-24.
5. Colossians 1:13-14.
6. Billy Joel, "Only the Good Die Young," copyright © 1977, JoelSongs.
7. See Genesis 3.
8. See C. S. Lewis, *The Lion, the Witch and the Wardrobe* (New York: HarperCollins, 1978).
9. *The Shawshank Redemption,* directed by Frank Darabont (Beverly Hills, CA: Castle Rock Entertainment, 1994).
10. *The Shawshank Redemption.*

Chapter 10

1. Romans 6:6-7,11.
2. Romans 8:13.
3. Colossians 3:5-7.
4. Romans 7:24.
5. James McBride, *The Color of Water: A Black Man's Tribute to His White Mother* (New York: Riverhead Books, 1996), 2.
6. Luke 9:62.
7. Matthew 10:16-17,22,34-39.
8. See John 21:1-17.
9. John 21:18.
10. John 21:19.
11. For more information, read the "I Have a Dream" speech Dr. Martin Luther King Jr. delivered on the steps of the Lincoln Memorial in Washington, D.C., on August 28, 1963. A copy of the speech can be

found online at www.stanford.edu/group/King/publications/speeches/
address_at_march_on_washington.pdf.
12. Luke 4:18.

Chapter 11

1. *Forrest Gump,* directed by Robert Zemeckis (Hollywood: Paramount, 1994).
2. James 1:2.
3. Hebrews 9:27, KJV.
4. James 4:13-15.
5. There is one possible exception to the inevitability of physical death. Those children of God who are still alive when Christ returns will be caught up in the air to meet their Savior. But even those who are alive at that time will have an appointment with God.

To learn more about WaterBrook Press and view
our catalog of products, log on to our Web site:
www.waterbrookpress.com